Murder

In The

Village Library

By Collett, Fogarty,

and Webner

Dedicated to the loyal patrons of The Village Library, its wonderful volunteers, and bibliophiles everywhere.

"People can lose their lives in libraries. They should be warned."

Saul Bellow

PROLOGUE

SAVANNAH, GEORGIA

THURSDAY, AUGUST 6, 2015

It was all Molly could think of at first - what was the poor woman's hemoglobin - perhaps 12.8? The blood looked rich enough. Obviously not oxygenated well. Too dark. Nonetheless, a nice lush color of deep scarlet with a hue of blue velvet now well settled over all. The spillage was massive and had oozed down the corridor hugging the edge between wall and highly polished wooden flooring, heading across the width of the flat plane and making a distinct current down the hall to the new wing.

God knows who is going to clean up this mess, thought Molly.

The body was wedged very haphazardly half way down the corridor in the corner between the wall and the comfy reading sofa. The plastic Ficus tree with pseudo Spanish moss at the base had been knocked over.

Molly had almost tripped over the thing on her route through the library to turn on the lights. She had been looking out of the windows in the back as she made her way down the hall leading to the non-fiction section.

Once she had seen an alligator in the lagoon behind the library. All she could see this morning were the lily pads floating on the glassy surface of the lagoon. She continued looking at the lagoon as she walked. Suddenly her foot bumped into something on the floor in the hall.

Quite unexpectedly Molly's mind pondered on the exact color red in one of the paintings that covered the corridor walls. She couldn't help herself; the blood was such an exact match. However she knew the subconscious mind always took over in these precarious situations dredging up nutty, trivial stuff you would normally never admit out loud. Like last week when she thought she saw someone who looked vaguely like Tommy Petroff wandering around the library. But Tommy was dead. She had been busy helping library patrons and when she was finished the man was gone. Just her vivid imagination. It had to be. How could she recognize him after twenty-five years? Was that even possible? The mind takes over in these dubious situations, just walks all over your conscious mind and brings forth insane stuff you would normally never think of.

Molly, a trauma surgeon in her former life, now older than most, at five feet two, was dressed in her usual uniform, khakis, blue button down shirt and Sperry boat shoes. Her mouth hung ajar in mortification. Did she need to bend down to the woman's neck to feel for a pulse? One dead eye stared up at Molly. She decided against the drill of determining life . . . or not. "Or not" was quite obvious.

Only two minutes after arriving, Molly, quite surprised to find the library unlocked, continued about her routine of turning on the lights and booting up the computers. She had almost tripped over the body of the woman.

The dead woman's head looked like an explosion of blood and brain matter. A splatter of blood clung to the wall at standing height. No murder weapon in sight.

My name tag, I need my name tag Molly thought, unaided by anything other than triviality at a time of complete mind-bending, heart-rending shock. Then her lifelong training kicked in and she stepped forward, deftly avoiding the blood, leaned down and studied the scene. The woman's clothes stuck to her as if damp. Blood had joined forces with the dampness, diluting the blood which had penetrated the weave of the deceased's Eileen Fisher blouse. Badly timed, sweat began to bead and fall freely off her forehead down to mingle with the red blood cells.

Her own heartbeat was audible in her ears – thump, thump, thump-thump – please don't let her go into supraventricular tachycardia right now. This just wasn't the time! She ignored that thought, fumbling to get out her iPhone 6 with which she snapped the entire body from various angles. Then she followed the congealing blood flow toward the Dewey Decimal wing, snapping shots with her phone while carefully avoiding the mess.

Molly's mind raced. This must have occurred last night. The blood is coagulated and smelling of ferrous sulphate and recently dead body tissue.

As she gazed once again upon the woman's body, Molly thought she recognized her. No, there were over ninety volunteers working at the Village Library. How could she know every last one of them? On the other hand, perhaps she did. Molly peered closer. Molly noticed an exquisite Harry Winston ring on the woman's right fourth finger, quite obvious as the dead woman's arm sprawled out to the side giving Molly an exceptional view of the ring. She'd seen that rock before.

Didn't that complete airhead wife of Tommy Petroff's flaunt such a distinctive ring in Molly's face at a party years ago? Molly's mind jolted like an electrical current back to that party.

"Oh Molly, you're an Emergency Room nurse, you poor dear. It will be a long time before you see a ring like mine . . ." She had waved the ring in Molly's face and Molly had wanted to take out her eyes without benefit of anesthesia.

Molly sincerely hoped this was not that ring . . . otherwise this body would be of that woman, ex-wife of Tommy Petroff. How long has it been since I've seen the Petroffs? It must be at least twenty years.

She leaned against the "Rental" bookshelves because she felt quite light-headed. When she put her hand back to steady herself on top of the short book shelf, she felt the bronze statue of a child sitting reading a book. Molly pulled back her hand immediately because the statue was wet and sticky. Then she looked at her hand. Sulphuric, dark red blood stuck to her hand like a second skin.

Damnation, do something Molly. Call Security.

While Molly waited for Security, she wondered who had been working the last shift yesterday. God forbid the dead body is Laura Petroff because that would open a Pandora's Box.

Only when she heard Security pull up in front did her eyes drift to an iPad resting by a computer on the desk. Who would leave an iPad behind? Could it belong to that poor woman in the hall?

* * *

Donato Santorelli, whom everyone called Dash, a particularly persnickety and detail-oriented Security guy squealed the tires as he swung his security vehicle into a library parking space.

Molly stood by the statue until the island Security guy burst through the front door. "I think I know who it is," hissed Molly through clenched teeth. She held out her bloody hand and pointed to the body.

Dash looked to where she pointed. One look and he knew this was no accident.

THE PREVIOUS DAY

August being the month of excessive heat and humidity, many people left the island to appreciate a more temperate climate. Laura Banderas worked her regular shift on Wednesday at the entirely volunteer-run library as usual. The Village Library offered 30,000 volumes to be borrowed, read, inhaled and loved. The island residents treasured this gem of a library due to its convenience and the amiability and helpfulness of its volunteers.

Her 2:30 to 5:00 PM shift proved to be boring. She worked with her neighbor Merilee MacKenzie. Laura didn't like working with her. In fact, she couldn't think of anyone who liked to work with her. Merilee had two very annoying traits. She would whisper gossip to you even though there wasn't another soul in the building. When she wasn't whispering, she would talk to your face in a normal tone but her eyes would be closed as if she were reading from a teleprompter projected on the inside of her eyelids.

Otherwise the shift went smoothly. Smoothly perhaps did not exactly say it all. Patrons returned books that hadn't been checked out. Some patrons swore they didn't owe a cent when told they had fines for books they had sworn they had returned. Laura then had to go to the shelves to see if the book had somehow made it back. One book, a Nelson DeMille thriller called "The Panther" was definitely on the shelf so Laura waived the fee graciously. In addition, an agitated patron had carried on quite badly saying how a white library card in his "rental

6

book", "Missoula: Rape And The Justice System in a College Town" by Jon Krakauer – absolutely gave him the right to keep the book for three weeks without charge and he wasn't going to "pay a goddamn cent." Laura withstood the outburst with a smile, admitting the library was at fault for not putting a green rental card in the rental book. She said, "The library is run by volunteers and we try to do our best."

"Obviously your best isn't good enough," shouted the man as he did an about face and left the library.

Laura sighed. She thought she heard snickering coming from somewhere in the stacks.

Volunteers were trained to be polite and gracious to every patron. Despite the training, Laura felt she should get a medal for dealing with that last patron. In her younger, more attractive days, Laura would have told the guy he was a royal pain in the ass just like her ex-husband, Tommy Petroff. Tommy had been a lying, alcoholic, adulterous sociopath as well as a perfected psychological torturer. He never hit her but if words could kill, she'd be lying dead years ago.

Around 4 PM, Laura stood by the back window looking at the lily-pad filled lagoon. The rain coming quickly now, obscured everything on the lagoon. Thunder and lightning added drama. She hoped the rain would be done by 5 PM when they closed up. Closing the library did not just involve walking out the door:

- computers had to be turned off,
- lights had to be out,
- the desk needed to be straightened up,

7

- returned books had to be placed on their appropriate shelves,
- stacks had to be checked to make sure no children (or adults) were lingering,
- doors had to be locked; the front door, the door in the children's room, the lagoon doors, and the door in the hallway.

Volunteers exited from the back door which automatically locked after them.

At 5 PM the rain was still raging like there was no tomorrow. Merilee had left early complaining of painful back spasms. She limped out the front door and made a determined dash through the torrent of rain to her nearby car.

After she turned the lights off, Laura left by the back door. She streaked across the grass to where her car sat under a Live Oak – thankfully the tree hadn't dropped any branches which they were wont to do in the slightest wind. Forgetting her original plan to stop at Publix for milk, Laura started up her car, turned the windshield wipers on dramatically fast, and headed for the Deer Creek gate.

Of course, right then she remembered her iPad resting on the library desk next to the computer. The thought of leaving her 300 downloaded books behind and not being able to read herself to sleep with her latest gripping selection was almost too much to bear. Laura had no key to get back into the library, but the Library

President lived nearby and she had a key. So Laura started to make a "U" turn when she saw the digital time print-out on her dashboard.

Yes! It was only 5:15 PM and the pharmacy was still open. They kept a key volunteers used to open in the mornings.

Laura parked by the pharmacy. As she turned off the engine, she remembered quite clearly she hadn't locked the front door after Merilee left. She drove back to the library through the rain and thunder.

She parked in front of the library and made a mad charge for the door and pushed it open.

PART I

CHAPTER 1

NEW YORK CITY

MONDAY, APRIL 15, 1991

Bob Hathaway read the New York Times by folding it lengthwise so that it didn't encroach on his seatmate's space. It was early Monday morning. He always caught the 7:06 Metro North train out of South Norwalk so that he could make it to his office in The City before 9 AM. He wanted to be the first associate to start work. He had plenty of work.

Nevertheless, as usual, the Metro North train slowed near the Cos Cob power plant. The lights dimmed. There wasn't enough sunlight this early in the morning to continue reading.

"Here we go again." he said to the elegantly dressed woman who had boarded the train at Greenwich. She seemed to Bob as though she should be riding in the back seat of a Lincoln Town car, not on a dirty Metro North train car. She glanced at him with a frosty glare and didn't comment. Well, he thought, no one wants to chat with a complete stranger this early in the morning. The train came to a screeching, shuddering halt.

"Someday they will fix the electric system so that we can get to Grand Central on time." he commented, even though he didn't expect a response from the lady.

"Do you take this train every day?" she asked out of the blue.

Surprised by the unexpected words, he folded his newspaper, stuffed it in his leather Coach brief case and said "Yes, unless I'm on my way to LaGuardia for a quick trip down to D.C." Bob instantly recalled the elevator trip with Richard Rosen, a/k/a Stinky, when he suggested in no uncertain terms that Bob should replace his hard-sided Samsonite briefcase with something more upscale. Rosen glanced at the saddle tan Coach leather briefcase he carried.

"What do you do?" she asked.

Her question jolted Bob back to the present and he said, "I work at a law firm in The City."

Bob was a little below average height at about five foot eight. He had put on quite a bit of weight since school due to lack of exercise and a fondness for rich food. His reddish hair, round face, and blue eyes reflected his Scandinavian heritage.

*   *   *

After law school he landed a job with the Alaska Attorney General in Juneau. He didn't like the work and he didn't like Alaska. After a year he quit to join a law firm in New York City. He found the change from Alaska to Manhattan a shock because he was not outgoing and

11

therefore had difficulty landing clients. Bob hated his current job and he didn't like the people in the firm because they made fun of his Midwest accent and upbringing.

He had overheard some of the other associates in the break room discussing a party at the Harvard Club over the weekend. Chip sniggered and nudged Doug, "It's no wonder the back woods boy has no clients . . ." Smirk. Smirk. Snigger. Laugh. Laugh.

I would be happier fly fishing on a trout stream than dancing at a club in South Norwalk Bob thought as he quietly slipped away. Bob wondered if they were right. He came to the sudden realization that his career wasn't going anywhere. Bob, in his sixth year as an associate at a small law firm with offices on West 46th street, knew sixth year associates rarely made partner. Maybe he just wasn't cut out for the law.

He was trying to pay back his student loans while hoping against hope that soon he might make partner. He had married Molly Cohen after relocating to the northeast. Molly worked the night shift at the Norwalk Hospital on Old Norwalk road, only a few miles from their condo. She worked the night shift because it paid more and she and Bob could use the extra income. She also had loans from the College of Medicine and Dentistry of New Jersey. Bob, too, had student loans to pay back. Molly drove Bob to the station in the morning and picked him up at night in the same old AMC Pacer she had driven to school in Newark. Other than those few minutes they didn't see much of each other.

The lady looked out the window as the train began to move. A few minutes later the train stopped at the 125th street station. Bob noticed no one ever got on or off at this station. He wondered why they bothered to stop here. The doors closed quickly and the train started to move again with a jolt. It began the slow decent into the underground portion of the trip.

As the 7:06 pulled into the lower level of the terminal, the passengers stood up facing the doors. It was as if they didn't get up and quickly get out they would spend the rest of their lives on that train. Grabbing his briefcase, Bob moved to the door with the woman. The doors opened and a thousand people jostled each other as they began their long walk down the platform in semi darkness.

Bob shot his cuff and glanced at his watch as he entered the main terminal. It showed 8:23 so he knew he had enough time for a leisurely walk to his office. He walked up the stairs leading to the Met Life building and then through the open air passage beneath the Helmsley building, exiting on East 46th street.

* * *

Laura Petroff watched as Bob Hathaway climbed the stairs on his way out of Grand Central. She walked out of the terminal onto Vanderbilt Avenue and caught a taxi to the offices of Petroff Enterprises. She was headed for another one of their tedious board meetings. Laura rarely participated actively in the board meetings. She attended only because most of the stock in Petroff Enterprises was in her name. Putting the stock in her name was a device to protect her shares from attack by disgruntled investors should any ever materialize. She did not understand business and found spending money far more interesting than making it. She hoped the meeting would be brief so she could return to Connecticut for her tennis lessons at the Greenwich Country Club after which she had to prepare for a party at the couple's mansion located on Merriebrook Lane just south of the Merritt Parkway in Greenwich.

The mansion on Merriebrook Lane had been purchased by Tommy, Laura's husband, two years earlier. A Fortune Five Hundred company had used it for executive retreats and as a comfortable place for high level out of town executives while they attended corporate meetings in Stamford. The property, known as Treetops, included 7 bedrooms, a billiard room, library, living room, large banquet room in the main building, an artist's studio in a separate building and nearly one hundred acres of prime land in Greenwich and Stamford. An adjacent building held living space for three full time staff. The grounds boasted a swimming pool, a tennis court, formal gardens and two greenhouses. Before becoming a corporate retreat, Treetops had been the home of Libby Holman, a Broadway singer from the early 1930's. The Petroffs frequently held lavish parties for friends and potential investors at Treetops. Like most of their assets, the property was titled in Laura's name.

CHAPTER 2

Laura was the only child of Seymour and Dorothy Higginbottom. She grew up in the small town of Gnadenhutten on the Tuscarawas River in Ohio. Seymour owned and operated a funeral parlor. The Higginbottoms were not rich, but comfortable. She earned straight "A's" at Indian Valley Local and was Valedictorian of her class. She was a cheerleader all four years in high school and captain her senior year. She sang in the choir, participated on the debate team, and played piano in the school's orchestra.

She remembered going to the state basketball championship in her junior year. The cheerleaders were lined up in two lines on each side of the doors of the Indian Valley yellow school bus. As each team member jogged up to the bus, pompoms waved and shook and cheers filled the late afternoon air. The basketball team members were followed by the trainers, school administrators, and cheerleaders. The cheerleaders boarded last and as they walked to the back where they always rode, Chuck, the team captain, touched Laura's hand in passing and asked if she would sit with him on the way home. She smiled and continued to the back with an almost imperceptible nod of her bouncy curls.

The doors of the bus closed with a pneumatic hiss. The driver, as he shifted gears and headed north on Interstate 70 to Canton, fifty miles north, smiled to himself as he inhaled the familiar aroma of teenage testosterone, Old Spice, and the slight waft of Wind Song.

16

The game between the Indian Valley Braves and St. Thomas Aquinas was within a few points throughout the first, second and third quarters. When the fourth quarter began the Braves seemed to be a different team. Their fans roared. Chuck couldn't miss a basket from any spot on the floor which disoriented St. Thomas. In a panic, they took shot after shot that they shouldn't have taken. Every one was an air ball.

As the clock wound down to a little over two minutes in the fourth quarter, Indian Valley was ahead by twelve points. St. Thomas Aquinas took their last time out. When they returned to the court Tommy Petroff took the in-bound throw and went straight to the basket. The St. Thomas Aquinas fans jumped to their feet and screamed. After Tommy made that two-pointer he never looked back. Each time Indian Valley got possession of the ball, he stripped it away. He scored two three-point field goals and another two pointer. With only three seconds left on the clock the score was tied. Chuck fouled Tommy Petroff. Tommy coolly took his place at the line and with nonchalance dropped two free throws to win the game for St. Thomas Aquinas by two points. As Tommy turned to go back to his jubilant team and coach, he stopped mid-court. He looked directly into Laura Higginbottom's eyes, performed a courtly bow to her, and blew her a kiss.

Laura walked to the back of the bus looking for Chuck and an empty seat beside him. However, she found Chuck in a window seat staring into the darkness outside the bus. Next to him was Jeff, his best friend.

The bus ride home to Gnadenhutten was quiet and somber. The next day at school Laura asked Chuck what he was so upset about. He unsmilingly bowed to her and blew her a kiss. Laura finally persuaded Chuck that she has never seen "that Petroff boy" in her entire life and that she had no idea why he had singled her out. They continued their courtship and were elected King and Queen of the Senior Spring Prom the following year.

In her senior year she applied to colleges and was accepted at The Ohio State University in Columbus, Ohio; Mount Union College in Alliance, Ohio; and Boston University. Laura chose BU because she wanted to be as far away from "nowhere-Ville" as possible and to forget the small town, rural life she had led for eighteen years. She majored in Fashion Design and minored in searching for a rich or potentially rich husband.

In the spring of her first year at college she met Tommy Petroff again at a mixer sponsored by Tommy's fraternity, Kappa Sigma. She recognized Tommy from his gallant gesture after his team won the AA state championship three years before.

Tommy was attending Boston University on an academic scholarship studying Computer Science. He grew up in the small town of Louisville in southern Ohio. His father died when he was twelve and he was raised by his mother and an aunt. His mother was the assistant produce manager at the local Walmart and would not have been able to afford to send him to BU without the scholarship. Tommy was bright and ambitious. He did not have to work hard in college and spent most of his

18

time at parties and meeting people who might become important to him later in his career. He dropped out of school in his third year and began to dabble in business, most of which involved selling merchandise. Laura dropped out of school the same year and married Tommy in her hometown.

CHAPTER 3

Bob Hathaway crossed Vanderbilt and Madison and walked into the Dunkin Donuts in the next block. He bought a medium sized black coffee and continued west on 46th crossing 5th Avenue. His office was in the next block and by now the sidewalks were getting crowded.

Thank god I don't have to take a subway downtown, he thought.

The offices of Wormslow & Simpson LLP occupied the 44th, 45th, and 46th floors of the Capital One building. Bob took the express elevator to the reception area on the 44th. The receptionist, Malinda Coleman, told him that he was to attend an important meeting in conference room C on the 46th floor at 9:30. He took out his security card and proceeded through the double frosted glass doors. Associate attorneys did not have offices at W&S, not even six-year associates. He and all of the other associates and paralegals worked in cubicles, although the associates' cubicles were slightly larger than the paralegals' cubicles. He sat at his desk and checked his in box as he unpacked his briefcase. His coffee was cold so he went to the break room and dumped it. He knew there would be coffee and maybe pastries at the meeting.

* * *

All of the other senior associates sat around the large mahogany conference table. Bob sat next to Howard Turner, another six-year associate. Before they could finish the small talk, the managing partner Richard Rosen entered the room. Everyone called him Mr. Stinky behind his back because he always wore too much cologne. Stinky began by telling the crowd that the past year had been bad in terms of income. Associates were not billing enough hours. As a result of this the partners decided that no associates would be elevated to partner this year. That message was greeted with a subdued moan.

"This meeting is over. Return to your offices." said Stinky. As they were all preparing to leave, Stinky barked, "Hathaway, stay behind."

Bob remained seated and Stinky waited until the last of the group had left and closed the door. Then he sat down next to Bob and said. "Bob, I know that my announcement must have disappointed you. But I can offer you a job as a permanent associate if you care to remain with the firm. You don't have to give me your answer now. Tomorrow will be soon enough. In addition, I want you to work with Bradley on a new credit agreement that Colonial America is considering. This is a very important deal and I don't want any screw ups. Understand?"

Bob nodded his head in agreement.

"Do you understand?" repeated Stinky in a louder voice.

"Yes" said Bob.

"Bradley is waiting for you in his office. Now go!" Stinky strode out of the conference room leaving the door open and the stench of his cologne behind.

Bob hated Bradley Morrison III. Bradley was a junior partner. He was one of the most egotistical and arrogant attorneys in the firm. In addition, he was a liar. He took credit for anything worthwhile that the associates did.

Bob took the circular stair case down two flights and walked into Morrison's office after the secretary motioned him in.

Bradley Morrison was a partner so he got an office with an actual door and a window. His office looked out over 46th street toward the park, but one couldn't see the park because of other taller buildings in the way. He had a mahogany desk, an oriental carpet over the standard office carpeting, and some yachting pictures on his wall next to his framed diplomas and memberships testifying to his right to practice before various courts. When Bob entered, Morrison, dressed in his usual starched white shirt with suspenders and matching bright bow tie. He was on the phone and waved Bob toward a chair in front of his desk. When he finished his call, Bradley explained to Bob that they had been assigned to work on a deal for their client Colonial American Bank and Trust. Bradley said, "The bank is negotiating a $400 million line of credit for an outfit called Petroff Enterprises. Unfortunately, I'm completely swamped with work on the pharmaceutical merger so I'm not going to be able to give you much help. Handle it. But don't screw it up."

Typical. I do the all the work and Bradley takes all the credit, thought Bob.

CHAPTER 4

Tommy Petroff attended Boston University on an athletic scholarship, but dropped out after his third year. Then he went to work for Barneys New York. Back then it was located on 7th avenue between 16th and 17th street. He imported men's clothing. He learned the business quickly and began importing and selling apparel on his own as a side business. Of course, when Barneys learned of his personal activities, they fired him.

After losing his job at Barneys, he founded Petroff Enterprises. The concept was fairly simple. The company purchased inexpensive apparel, mostly name brand "knock-offs" made in India and Bangladesh. It imported them into the United States and resold them to mid-range retail stores at three to four times the cost. Petroff Enterprises had a subsidiary, TP Logistics, which managed warehouses on the east and west coasts.

Entrepreneur Tommy had the gift of gab. He was an expert at talking people into investing in his business. Now, after several years, Petroff Enterprises was flourishing. Many of its early investors were delighted with the returns they had earned. Tommy promised his investors a high, but not a suspiciously high, rate of return. And they received it. Word spread and new investors lined up to give Tommy Petroff their money. The investors included money managers, pension funds, wealthy individuals and some greedy, but not so wealthy investors. Over the first five years of its existence Petroff had grown its revenues from three million a year to a staggering forty-six million dollars a year. All looked good. Recently, Business Week had put Tommy on its cover and had an in-depth article about his successful companies. The response to the article was a new influx of investors.

Tommy's company was flying high. It was almost drowning in money from greedy investors. He would submit invoices from fictitious companies for fees relating to accounting, logistics and other services that were never rendered. Petroff Enterprises paid these invoices by depositing money into Tommy's offshore accounts in Lichtenstein and in Panama. Sandra Cummings, CFO of Petroff Enterprises, couldn't help but notice the large payments to vendors who seemed to be invisible and provide no goods or services. Her relationship with Tommy insured that she would never raise any flags.

Tommy soon realized that having the money in accounts on different continents was not convenient. He decided to purchase investment grade diamonds from vendors on 47th street in New York. The diamonds would be easy to keep hidden and easy to move in an emergency.

Almost every month he would buy $50,000 to $100,000 worth of diamonds. He was careful to purchase from several different sellers and never more than a dozen stones at a time. The sellers, who received wire transfers to pay for the diamonds, were only too happy to serve this regular and extravagant client. All the diamonds were investment grade weighing in at between one and three karats, each worth $15,000 at a minimum. Over the years,

Tommy accumulated almost two hundred of these gems. He didn't tell anyone about the diamonds, not even Laura.

Next he needed a place to hide them for a rainy day. He didn't want to fool around with a safety deposit box at a bank because he wanted to be able to get to them on a moment's notice.

One day while walking through his living room he noticed the sculpture of a child reading a book that Laura had purchased from Javier. Javier Banderas was a so-called sculptor Laura had invited to live in the studio on their property. If that guy's a sculptor, then I'm a nuclear physicist.

Tommy had never paid much attention to Laura's art work, but this time he picked up the statue and examined it looking for a signature. The base was covered with felt. He peeled back a corner of the felt searching for the signature. Instead he found a large cavity. Wow. What a great place to stash my diamonds. Pleased with his inspection he put the sculpture back on the table in the living room.

Lately, Petroff Enterprises was experiencing a decline in sales. Tommy knew he had to expand. DVD devices were starting to appear on the market and they were being embraced by the public as an alternative to VCR players. Tommy could see that it was just a matter of time before prerecorded material would be on DVDs instead of VHS tapes. Tommy planned to travel to China and, with the help of some friends he had met at his frequent parties, he hoped to line up a supplier of DVD players. But, unlike the apparel, the cost of these products required more cash than he had available.

The board of Petroff Enterprises consisted only of Tommy, his wife Laura and Sandra Cummings, his chief financial officer. Tommy persuaded his board of directors to authorize him to negotiate a $400 million line of credit with Saul Goldsmith, Executive Vice President of Colonial America Bank and Trust. The loan was to be partially secured by the stock of TP Logistics, Petroff's warehouse subsidiary, as well as the warehouse inventory. The line of credit would be used by Tommy to expand his business into consumer electronics and to add to his growing personal wealth. The bank was delighted to make the loan because Petroff Enterprises was willing to pay four percentage points above the current prime rate.

The board meeting had just wrapped up when Tommy looked over at Sandra Cummings and asked, "How are we doing with payments to our investors?" Sandra looked at her briefing book and then flipped through a stack of computer print outs. She stated all payments that were due had been paid on time. However, because of the increase in investments and lower sales, there would be difficulty in repaying any more investors. Tommy's plans always included an element of high risk.

CHAPTER 5

FRIDAY, APRIL 26, 1991

Tommy met Saul Goldsmith for lunch at the Four Seasons on East 57th to work out the general terms of the transaction. Tommy was charming. He made his pitch about his idea to buy DVD players manufactured in China and sell them to Nobody Beats the Wiz, Best Buy, Target and other large electronics stores. The deal meant a lot to the bank and Saul wanted to conclude it as quickly as possible. They agreed on the interest rate but didn't discuss details. Those would be left up to the lawyers.

After lunch, Tommy asked, "What is the next step?"

Saul replied that he would have the bank's attorneys draw up the papers.

Tommy said "Send them to my attorney, Zack Prestowitz at Compton & Wright."

Bob Hathaway, attorney for the bank, prepared drafts of the agreements and sent them to Zack Prestowitz. Zack reviewed the preliminary drafts and made many changes. He sent the revised draft back to Hathaway by messenger. That started a long tedious series of phone calls between the attorneys. Bob didn't like working with Prestowitz. Nearly every comment or suggestion Bob made was rejected by Prestowitz. Prestowitz was not willing to provide Bob with the detailed information about the collateral that would normally be expected as part of the deal. Instead, Prestowitz gave Bob printouts of the inventory he said was in the warehouses. Ordinarily, Bob would have insisted on an on-site inspection but Prestowitz said it would take too much time and they were under pressure to finalize the deal.

Bob reported his feelings and lack of progress to Bradley. Bradley, red in the face and pounding his fist shouted, "Get the deal done! Saul wants it done! And you will get it done!"

The closing was scheduled for August 2nd at Prestowitz's office.

FRIDAY, AUGUST 2, 1991

Tommy and Sandra were ushered into the main conference room where paralegals had spread neat stacks of documents around a large conference table. After Zack and Bob reviewed the final documents, the principals sat down and were shown where to sign.

After all of the documents were signed, and everyone had left the room but Bob and Tommy, Tommy came up to Bob and said, "I want to thank you for helping make this deal move along. You seemed to work well with Zack. Not everyone does."

"By the way, I'm having a small party tomorrow night and I would like you to attend. You're welcome to bring a guest. Nothing formal, just cocktails at 7 and dinner at 9. Some of my good friends and acquaintances will be there."

Bob said, "I'll check with my wife, Molly, and call you back and let you know.

CHAPTER 6

GREENWICH, CONNECTICUT

SATURDAY, AUGUST 3, 1991

It was very dark by the time Bob, with Molly sitting beside him, drove their eight-year old AMC Pacer onto the Merritt Parkway heading for Greenwich. Molly didn't say much and was clearly feeling uncomfortable at the prospect of attending a party where she was certain she wouldn't know a soul. Bob was excited to see where Tommy lived. He had heard so much about the Treetops estate. He also hoped to meet some real high rollers. Maybe he could line up an important client for the firm and still have a chance to become a partner.

The Parkway was a four-lane divided road and trucks were not allowed. The twisting, turning road had no shoulder, no street lights and very short perilous on and off ramps. That didn't stop drivers from racing along at twenty miles an hour over the legal limit of fifty. Bob got off the parkway at Den Road. After making several wrong turns due to the darkness and lack of street signs, he finally found Merriebrook Lane.

Large brick homes lined both sides of the lane. Each was set back a good distance from the road and behind low rock walls. So typical of Connecticut. He came to a small bridge with a sign that read:

TREETOPS
PRIVATE ROAD

He crossed the small bridge and drove up the private drive that led to Treetops. The road was paved, but narrow and had no lights. It seemed to have been cut out of a forest of enormous trees. Soon they came to the top of a hill and could see a three story brick house ahead lit by flood lights. The grand white colonial appeared to be floating in a black void.

Bob cringed when he thought about their car. Most people he knew had two cars. If they had kids one would be a late model Volvo station wagon or a Range Rover. If they didn't have kids, one would be a BMW or a Saab convertible. The second car was called a station car, usually an old American compact. It ran well but looked like a piece of junk with faded paint and some rust. They could park it all day at the commuter rail station without worrying about it being stolen. No one would want it.

He and Molly only had one car, the eight year old lime green Pacer she had purchased used while in medical school. He decided that if anyone should comment on it, he would tell them that their Beemer was at the dealership being serviced and they were using their station car.

He gave his car keys to the valet and they made their way up the slate walk leading to the front door. Bob reached for the brass knocker when the door suddenly opened. Framed by the light from the foyer behind her, stood Laura Petroff.

She said, "You must be the Hathaways."

Molly said "Yes, I'm Molly Cohen and this is my husband Bob Hathaway."

"I am very pleased to meet you Molly." She extended her hand to Molly flashing a large diamond ring. It looked to Molly like the 'Sunflower' ring that had been featured in a Harry Winston advertisement in the Times. It must be worth six figures.

"Come in. It's nice to see you again Bob."

Molly shot Bob a quick look.

"You're the last to arrive." said Laura

"Bob had some difficulty finding the right street." Molly commented archly.

"That is not surprising. This part of Greenwich can be very confusing at night. Before I introduce you to the other guests, let me show you around a little." Laura moved back and ushered them inside.

She led them out of the large foyer into what must be called the library. The room had windows on two walls, a fireplace and built-in book shelves from floor to ceiling on the other wall complete with a library ladder to reach the top shelves. In the center there were four facing chairs upholstered in a green paisley fabric arranged around a small coffee table. There were two gold brocade wing back chairs facing each other on either side of the fireplace flanked by Chippendale end tables. In front of the south facing window was a large George III mahogany desk with a leather inset. Completing the look, sat a leather bound dictionary on a stand and off to the side stood a game table made of exotic inlaid wood. Molly gazed amazingly at the leather bound books that lined the shelves. She loved books and would give anything for a room like this.

"This house has an interesting history," said Laura, "It was originally built by Libby Holman who was a famous torch singer in the 1930s and 40s. Her first husband was Zachary Smith Reynolds, heir to the R. J. Reynolds tobacco fortune. He was shot dead. Some believed Libby murdered him. She was indicted for the murder, but the Reynolds family persuaded authorities to drop the charges and the death was ruled a suicide. Her second husband, Ralph Holmes, committed suicide."

"Michael Todd proposed to Elizabeth Taylor in this very room. She entertained Montgomery Clift, Turman Capote, Tallulah Bankhead, Imogene Coca, Martha Raye, Tennessee Williams among others. Libby married Louis Schanker in 1959. He was an artist and sculptor and their marriage was stormy. He was jealous of Libby's gay friends of both sexes and banned them from Treetops."

"Libby was found dead at the age of 67 in the garage slumped over in her Rolls-Royce. It was ruled another suicide, however, many of her friends, including Coretta Scott King, didn't believe it was a suicide. The ignition on the car was off and they believed Libby was too weak to close the garage door by herself. We still have the artist's studio on the property and now an artist in residence."

"That is very interesting" Molly said without conviction. "You have a lovely library. I love books. These look old and rare. Are any of them first editions?"

"I don't know if there are any first editions, but I know that most of the leather bindings are original and they look almost new. We purchased the entire collection when we bought the property from a corporation that owned Treetops for years. The corporation used it as a conference center."

"We acquired the forty acres in Stamford and seventy acres in Greenwich, plus the mansion and everything in it, the rugs, the paintings, the furniture, the china the silver . . . everything for less than twenty million. Then we sold most of the Greenwich property and made out like bandits because Tommy is such a good business man. We made sure we had enough of the land in Greenwich to keep the Greenwich address. There is nothing wrong with Stamford but . . . well . . . you know."

"When the corporation owned it, they employed four full time gardeners working in the two greenhouses. The gardeners had planted thousands of daffodils on the grounds. The corporation used to open the grounds to the public in May for the Daffodil Festival. After we bought it we got rid of the gardeners, closed the greenhouses and discontinued the Festival. I mean, you can't just have strangers walking around your property. Can you?"

"I've made many changes to the house, but I didn't change this room, because I always wanted a library. We made many of the changes because the house didn't fit our lifestyle. We entertain lavishly. We have so many friends and business acquaintances."

"We kept Libby's master bedroom and bath as they were because the bath is marble with a large fireplace and there is a Roman chaise in the center. It's terribly striking. I would like to show it to you," she said looking at Bob and smiling. "Perhaps some other time?"

She glanced at her watch and quickly added, "Please follow me."

CHAPTER 7

They entered a living room of majestic proportions. On one side there were windows that looked out the rear of the house over a manicured lawn and down a hill toward the Mianas river which was really only a small stream bordered by mature sugar maple trees. The wall opposite was decorated with original oil paintings, each illuminated by a light. The room was organized into several seating areas, each of which could accommodate a dozen people. There were several round and oval tables holding lamps, bowls, and even a small sculpture. In keeping with the rest of the house, the furniture was traditional. Three banquet-sized Persian rugs covered the floor.

Two groups of guests stood sipping drinks. The men gathered near the fireplace. The women stood by the windows looking at a sculpture of a child holding a book.

Two servants wearing white tops, black pants, and short aprons offered hors d'oeuvres on silver trays to Laura, Molly and Bob.

"I am sorry," said Laura to Bob and Molly. "Would you like a cocktail or something else? James can make almost anything." Molly said she would like white wine and Bob said he would like Knob Creek on the rocks. Laura stopped one of the servers and gave her the order. The servant returned quickly with their drinks. Laura linked her arm through Bob's arm and led him to a small group of men gathered by the fireplace. Molly followed, a slight frown on her face.

"Gentlemen, I'd like you to meet Bob Hathaway . . . Oh, and his wife Molly. This is Victor Banning, Javier Banderas, Sidney Collins, and Joe Yang. Victor is an investment banker from The City. Javier is our artist in residence, a gifted sculptor. You can see one of his works over there." She pointed to where the ladies stood admiring a small sculpture resting on a Queen Anne drop leaf table. The table was clearly an antique. "I'm sure you recognize Sidney as our congressional representative for the Fourth District. Joe is the US trade representative to China. Bob is an attorney in the city. Molly's a nurse."

"Excuse me," Molly straightened her shoulders. "I am a trauma surgeon practicing at Norwalk Hospital."

"Oh, I'm sorry, this is Dr. Cohen."

Joe gave a short bow. Victor extended his hand and both Molly and Bob shook it. Javier reached for Molly's hand and brought it to his lips.

"*Encantado*" Javier said with a big smile. He had an incorrigible interest in rich women. Aren't all doctors in America rich?

Victor turned to Bob and said, "I understand you're a lawyer with Wormslow & Simpson in the City. What kind of law do you practice?"

"I practice general business law, although most of my time recently has been in the financial area, corporate bonds, stock offerings and a little merger and acquisition work."

While the men talked, Molly, carrying her white wine, walked over to the three women standing around a table. A small bronze statue of a child reading a book

37

stood in the middle of the table. Molly introduced herself to the other women. They nodded, smiled and continued their conversation. Molly had no interest in the ladies' conversation which revolved around parties in Greenwich, tennis at the club, fund raisers, the polo tournament in Darian the next week, and other social topics. She drifted away from the ladies. She felt out of place. She wished she had not been talked into coming to this dinner party.

Molly stood all alone looking at an oil painting titled 'Rivage Vendeen' by André Bourrié. It depicted small cottages on a beach with sailboats. Molly found the painting peaceful. It distracted her from thinking about the dreadful party.

Just then Tommy Petroff, accompanied by a stunning woman in her early thirties with long red hair walked into the room. They approached Molly and Tommy introduced the woman as Sandra Cummings, his Chief Financial Officer. "Sandra, this is Dr. Molly Cohen. She's married to Bob Hathaway. Molly is a trauma surgeon who works at Norwalk hospital."

Molly was surprised that Tommy knew her position, especially after Laura had introduced her as a nurse. Molly smiled at Tommy.

Tommy returned her smile and said, "I have always respected physicians, especially those who operate on critical patients and save lives. Just imagine, Sandra, if you were in a terrible car accident and there were no trauma doctors to treat your life threatening injuries. We can't thank you enough for what you do, Molly."

Yolanda, one of the servants, entered the room and said, "Madam, dinner is served." She promptly left the room.

Laura turned to the guests, "Ladies and gentlemen, please follow me."

CHAPTER 8

The dining table rested on another large Serapi Persian rug. It was set with gleaming silverware, linen napkins, Baccarat crystal and large fresh flower arrangements. Crystal chandeliers hung over the table. A demilune console table held a large ice sculpture of a child reading a book lighted by an overhead pin point beam. The sculpture glittered like diamonds. Each place setting had a small hand blown glass vessel with a single rose and a place card.

Different wines were poured with each of the six courses. Sandra, Laura and Molly tasted each course, but didn't finish anything. Mrs. Banning and Mrs. Yang ate and drank everything that was placed before them and eyed the uneaten food hungrily. Mrs. Collins was far more interested in the wine than the food.

The more lively conversations seemed to be between Laura and Bob at one end of the table and Tommy and Molly at the other end. Tommy was his usual charming self. Molly, perhaps due to several glasses of wine, found herself enjoying Tommy's company.

Joe Yang droned on to the guests. " . . . China is undergoing a tremendous change. What was once a rural agricultural economy is becoming an urban manufacturing economy. It is reminiscent of the industrial revolution that took place in Europe in the 1800's. China used to make the fabric for apparel that was sent to the United States for finishing. Now China is making the cloth as well as the finished garments and shipping them to the

United States. As more people from rural areas move into the cities in search of better paying jobs, those jobs have to materialize. Factories are springing up all over. They already make many of the parts and components for machines manufactured in the United States. Before long they will be making washing machines, drill presses, furniture, and many other products and ship them to the US."

"Why is this happening?" asked Tommy.

"There are many reasons, but one of the biggest is that a factory worker in China earns about 20% of what a factory worker makes in the United States. That makes Chinese products significantly less expensive. There are other factors too."

Tommy said, "I've had some dealings with China's textile industry. Indeed, their costs are lower and their quality is improving. Joe, would you be able to set up some meetings for me with some Chinese technical companies?"

"Of course. What kind of companies?"

"I'm thinking of importing DVD recorders into the States," Tommy said.

Several of the women rolled their eyes and sighed. Business discussions always bored Laura too. She turned to her right, smiled at Javier and then looked at Bob while she tried to change the subject. "Did you see that bronze statue of the child reading a book in the living room? Javier created that. Did you notice the ice sculpture is a replica of your work, Javier? He is also making a large sculpture for the PepsiCo Sculpture Garden in Purchase. Javier is so talented and . . ."

"What's a DVD recorder?" interjected Sidney Collins.

"It's a device that can record digital information on a disk. Think of a video tape recorder and substitute a small disc for the tape. Some of you may have noticed that these days music is mostly recorded on CD's. CD's are small plastic discs about four and a half inches in diameter. DVD discs look the same but can hold much more information than a video tape, or even a CD. And DVD's don't deteriorate. People can record their own movies, pictures, music and even television programs," answered Tommy.

"Sure, I have contacts with some of those companies," said Joe Wang. "Most of them are located in Shenzhen in Guangdong province. It's on the coast of the South China Sea, just north of Hong Kong. Shenzhen is one of the world's fastest growing cities. Just let me know when you want to go."

Tommy turned to Molly and said "With your brains, not to mention your charm, you probably could have done practically anything and made truckloads of money. What motivated you to become a physician?"

"I was driving home one night on the Hutchinson River Parkway and I witnessed a terrible crash. I waited in my car while the EMTs rushed to assist the injured. I watched them risk their lives pulling people from the burning cars. It was then I decided I wanted to practice medicine. I wanted to do what I could to save lives. My

42

work has been very rewarding, but not in a financial sense . . . at least not yet."

Tommy smiled and lightly squeezed her arm.

Victor talked about investments.

Sidney talked about Washington, D.C. and the congress.

Javier talked about his latest sculpture project at the PepsiCo Corporation's Sculpture Garden in Purchase.

There was no dessert, much to the dismay of Mrs. Yang and Mrs. Banning.

"Coffee and after dinner drinks will be served in the living room," announced Tommy.

As the group rose and started to move toward the living room, Tommy approached Bob and asked him if he wouldn't mind chatting for a few minutes in the library. Bob sat in one of the gold wing back chairs and Tommy stood leaning against the desk. He handed Bob a snifter of Armagnac and offered him a cigar as he lit his own.

Taking in the aroma of the brandy he swirled it and began, "I am happy you and Molly were able to come tonight. I was impressed with your work on our line of credit deal. You may not know this but my company now employs over five thousand people in four states. We are doing well and the outlook is spectacular, especially when we get this electronics venture going. We don't have an in-house lawyer and we need one. I would like you to consider taking the position."

Bob was shocked. All he could think to say was, "Thank you for the compliment."

Tommy went on, "I am willing to pay $50,000 above what you are making now. But in addition, you would be entitled to 1,000 shares of Petroff Enterprises. Today the stock is probably worth four times your current annual salary. In a few years from now it will be worth ten times that much. What do you say?"

Bob paused for a long time as he thought about the money and he considered the prospect of working for an entrepreneur like Tommy instead of jerks like Stinky and Bradley.

Then he said, "Yes. I would like to work for you."

"Don't you want to talk it over with Molly?"

"No. She will agree as long as we don't have to relocate."

"There may be some travel involved, but no relocation my boy. You can work out of our office on Park Avenue."

They shook hands and rejoined the other guests in the living room. Tommy tapped his signet ring against his glass and the conversations stopped. "I want to introduce the newest member of Petroff Enterprises, Bob Hathaway, Vice President and General Counsel." While the guests clapped, Bob glanced at Molly. She wasn't clapping and she looked stunned.

As the party wound down and the guests prepared to leave, Javier approached Molly. "You must really visit the Donald Kendall Sculpture Garden in Purchase. We are currently installing one of my recent sculptures. Perhaps later this week?" he whispered.

"I don't know. Will you be there?"

"I wouldn't miss the opportunity to see a beautiful woman like you for anything. *Buenas Noches* my dear." He kissed her hand.

Molly was flattered and clearly enjoyed his attention. Then she noticed Laura kissing Bob on the cheek.

She walked over and said, "Good night Laura. I think my husband has had a little too much fun and a little too much to drink. Better give me the keys, Bob."

As they waited for their car to be delivered, Molly looked at Bob and said, "How do you know her?!!"

"Who?"

"Our hostess."

"She sat next to me on the train last week," said Bob.

Molly drove home in silence. Just before she turned into their driveway she said: "I don't like that woman. I want you to stay away from her."

"Molly, she's married to my new boss and she's a director of the company I'm going to work for," said Bob defensively.

"I want you to stay away from her." said Molly. "And another thing, don't make life decisions for both of us without talking to me."

CHAPTER 9

NEW YORK CITY

MONDAY, APRIL 20, 1992

Six weeks into his new job at Petroff Enterprises, Bob was floundering. He was used to working ten or more hours a day at his old firm. Even those ten hours were not enough to finish all of the work he did at W & S. Now he sat in his office staring out the windows at Park Avenue below. He realized he didn't have anything meaningful to do. Sure, he was making a lot more money, but he had assumed he would have plenty of duties and responsibilities to go along with the larger salary. Instead, he seemed to have a lot of time on his hands. He thought he could use the time to learn as much as he could about Petroff Enterprises while he had the time. So he did.

The following Monday, Bob Hathaway came to work with two things on his mind. Over the weekend, he had calculated he could pay off his and Molly's student loans by exercising some of his Petroff stock options. He was concerned about what he had learned about Petroff Enterprises and how it appeared to be paying off early investors with money from new investors. He decided to talk to Sandra Cummings about both issues. When he walked into Sandra's office, she was on the phone.

As she laid down the phone she said, "Hi Bob. Have a seat. What can I do for you?"

Bob sat down on the sofa behind a glass coffee table. He hadn't figured out how he was going to start this conversation. He knew Sandra was very loyal to Tommy and he didn't want to sound like he was suspicious of Tommy's business practices, but he was.

"Sandra, do you know some of Tommy's investors are complaining that they are not receiving the income they were promised?"

Sandra paused for a moment and then said, "There are always people who want more than they were promised."

"No." said Bob, "I have had calls and emails from people who have made investments and they say they are overdue for receiving the income promised. Some have threatened to sue. They have sent me their investment contracts and they look valid."

"Don't worry, Bob. We may just be a wee bit behind in making payments, but that's the way all investment companies work. You'll understand that after you have been with the company a little longer."

"OK, Sandra that's fine, but make sure you send their payments soon." said Bob. He was dissatisfied with her response. "By the way Sandra, how do I go about exercising some of my stock options? I want to pay off our student loans."

Sandra said, "My secretary can give you the forms, but with the company growing as fast as it is, you'll be giving up some future profits."

"I know, but these loans are like mill stones around our necks."

"Think about those future profits before you act hastily," Sandra iterated.

When Bob returned to his office with the stock forms, his secretary said he had a call from someone named Lars Larson from Duluth, Minnesota. Lars was Bob's roommate all three years in law school. After that they lost touch. They hadn't seen each other in years.

Bob called Lars back and learned that he was coming to New York on business. They arranged to have dinner together. He thought he would like to treat his old classmate to dinner at Daniel on East 65th, probably the most popular and expensive restaurant in New York. Sometimes one had to wait six months to get in. But when Bob's secretary mentioned Tommy's name she got the reservation he wanted.

Bob and Lars enjoyed a few cocktails at the bar while catching up. Lars had opened a one man legal office in Duluth and specialized in wills and estate planning. "Boring work and doesn't pay well but I like it. It leaves me plenty of time to play golf in the short summer, to go deer hunting in the fall, and to ice fish in winter.

They were seated at a small table for two against the wall. Lars ordered Bacon Wrapped Yellowfin Tuna. He was from the Midwest and any fresh fish was a treat. Bob ordered roasted wild Scottish grouse with sumac and black Mission figs.

Bob ordered a wine suggested by the sommelier with each course.

During dinner Bob said, "My new job is a lot different than what I did when I worked for Wormslow & Simpson. While I was there, they gave me plenty of work and I hardly had enough time to do it. At Petroff, my job is to keep everything in legal compliance, but I haven't the slightest idea of where to begin."

"You'll figure it out. You've only had the job a few months. Besides, I bet the money is a lot better."

The wine loosened Bob's tongue. "It is, but sometimes I wonder about the way Tommy runs the company." After a leisurely dinner, Bob picked up the check. The two old friends said good-bye. Lars returned to the St. Regis hotel and Tommy made his way to Grand Central to catch the train home.

CHAPTER 10

Sandra met with Tommy in his large corner office the morning after he returned from a business trip to China. After they finished going over the recent financial figures, Sandra said, "I had a strange meeting with Bob the other day. He said he was following up on complaints from some of our investors and he seemed troubled."

"We can't have him snooping around in that area. Next time he brings up the subject tell him that everything is under control and he should be spending more time learning his job, not trying to do yours," said Tommy.

On the contrary, Bob did not stop his inquiries. Over the next several weeks he logged on to the company server and started going through the financials even though he had been told that they were outside the scope of his job. He concluded Petroff Enterprises was a gigantic Ponzi scheme.

He arranged a meeting with Tommy to tell him what he had discovered. Tommy just brushed it off. He told Bob that there might have been some unusual investment strategies in the early days of the company, but all that had been straightened out.

Bob was not satisfied. He knew what he had seen.

THURSDAY, APRIL 23, 1992

A few days after their meeting, Tommy met with the head of Petroff's security. Lester (Les) Mazza was head of security and sometimes bodyguard for him. Tommy asked Les if he could tell what documents Bob had accessed. Les said he could identify everything Bob had accessed from his company computer. Tommy told Les Bob was becoming a problem and he could bring down the entire company if he continued snooping. Tommy worried that Bob might go to the authorities.

Les said, "That isn't likely. As the company attorney, he has an ethical duty to the company."

"Nevertheless," said Tommy, "we can't take the chance. I think we need to send him a strong message. My explanation and Sandra's warning didn't seem to end his prying."

"What do you want me to do Boss?"

"I want you to put a stop to his meddling," said Tommy.

* * *

Les Mazza had worked as a sergeant in the fortieth precinct in the Bronx before joining Petroff Enterprises. He was discharged from the NYPD for repeated complains about unnecessary use of force and the suspicion he was shaking down drug traffickers. He was never charged.

After he left Tommy's office, he went back to his own office, closed the door and dialed a number.

"Yeah?" said the person who answered.

"We need to meet" said Les. "Tonight at eleven at the Park Side Restaurant on 51st and Corona, across from the bocce courts."

At 10:30 PM Les parked his Lincoln Town Car on 51st across from the restaurant and walked across the street to watch the old Italian men play bocce in the park under the lights. At precisely 11:00 PM he walked in the door of the restaurant and looked around. It was practically empty, but in the far corner he spotted the man. Les could tell that he was a large man, probably over six feet tall and at least 250 pounds. He was wearing a black leather coat, despite the warm weather. He had short, wiry gray hair. Above his dark eyes was a single thick eyebrow. A scar on the right side of his face ran from his temple to his chin. The man had his back to the wall. Les walked over and took an empty seat at the table. The waiter had already set down two glasses of red wine, a basket of bread and antipasti on the table.

Les looked at the large, swarthy man and remembered when they were both police officers. For years they had profited from their own protection scheme. They would stop low level drug dealers and threaten to take them in unless the dealers agreed to share their earnings. Les and Sergei Romanoff had made thousands. It started to unravel when one of the dealers was arrested by a young new detective. The dealer told the DA all about Les and Sergei's protection racket in return for a reduced charge. Sergei and Les were investigated by internal affairs and eventually forced to resign.

Les started his own security firm. Eventually Tommy Petroff hired him to be his head of security. Sergei, found his true calling by becoming a fixer for anyone who could pay his fee. Over the years Sergei and Les stayed in touch.

Les said "I have a job for you."

"Yeah?" said Sergei.

"It has to look like an accident," said Les, as he pushed an envelope across the table. "Everything you need is in this envelope."

"What about the money?" said Sergei with a slight Russian accent.

"The money, his picture and his itinerary. It's all in the envelope." said Les. The mark will be visiting Washington D.C. on business next week. Do it then."

Sergei picked up the envelope in his left hand along with several pieces of antipasti with his right hand and left. Les paid the check and walked out. He stopped for a pistachio Italian ice from the Lemon Ice King across from where he parked his car.

CHAPTER 11

WASHINGTON, D.C.

MONDAY, APRIL 27, 1992

As Bob rode in the cab from Washington National Airport to his hotel, he wondered why Tommy had decided to send him to Washington for a legal seminar so suddenly. And, in particular, a seminar focused on Corporate Record Keeping. He also wondered why Les had insisted on driving him to La Guardia to catch the shuttle to D.C.

He thought back to the conversations he had with Sandra and Tommy regarding the irregularities that he had found. Maybe, just maybe, Tommy had taken Bob's word to heart and was sending him to this seminar as a first step to straightening his business out.

The cab pulled into the entry courtyard of the Four Seasons in Georgetown a few minutes after 4 in the afternoon. As Bob paid the cabbie, he decided he had time for a workout in the hotel's fitness center before showering, dressing, and going out to a restaurant across the street that Tommy had highly recommended. He might even have time for a drink at the hotel bar before dinner.

Bob lifted weights, ran on the treadmill, and sat in the sauna thinking about tomorrow's seminar. Upstairs a tall, well-muscled man entered the bar at the Four Seasons and sat at the bar. He looked into the convex mirrors above the smoked glass bar back. He watched the reflections of people entering the bar. The waiter brought a small silver bowl of mixed nuts and also one of warm olives. The man ordered a Tanqueray martini on the rocks. After his first sip, he pulled The Wall Street Journal out of his briefcase. As he folded the paper, his cell phone rang. A voice asked if the package had arrived. He smiled and responded in the affirmative.

The bartender noted that his customer was wearing a black leather coat and had an umbrella by his briefcase. When she brought a second martini to him she asked the big man if he thought it was going to rain. As if he had not heard the question the man told the bartender he was expecting a friend and placed his briefcase and umbrella on the seat next to him. The bartender went back to the end of the bar, pondering why anyone would be wearing a black leather coat when the temperature was in the eighties and carrying an umbrella when there wasn't a cloud in the sky.

Bob, freshly shaved and dressed, arrived in the bar at 6 PM. It was packed with the usual after work crowd of Washington power brokers, lawyers, and politicians. Bob could see only one empty seat at the far end of the bar. After wending his way through the crowd, he saw a briefcase and umbrella on the seat. As he turned to see if he could find another seat, he felt a tap on his shoulder. When he turned, he saw a mountain of a man remove the briefcase and umbrella from the seat and gesture to him to take it.

After Bob's Laphroaig single malt on the rocks was served, the two men struck up a conversation, introducing themselves to each other, inquiring where each was from and why they were in town. The man with the briefcase and umbrella told Bob that his name was Sergei Romanoff and that he was a head hunter in town for some interviews. They chatted for a while, discussing the hassles of traveling, the luxurious accommodations they were enjoying at the Four Seasons, and whether Bush or Clinton would win the Presidency in November. Bob didn't like to eat alone and asked Sergei if he would join him for dinner across the street at La Chaumiere. Sergei declined, telling him he had a flight home at 8 PM and was planning a late dinner with his wife in New York when he arrived.

They each had another drink and asked the bartender for their tabs. Sergei told Bob that he would walk to the corner with him and intercept a cab on its way to the Four Seasons. That way he could avoid tipping the doorman and the cabbie. They both chuckled and began walking toward the corner of 28th Street and M Street where Sergei could hail a cab and Bob would cross M Street to La Chaumiere.

As they stood on the corner waiting for the light to change, they said their goodbyes to each other. The light changed and Bob stepped off the curb. As he stepped, he felt a twinge in his thigh, but continued hurrying to the other side of the busy intersection watching the seconds tick down on the pedestrian crossing sign. Before he went into the La Chaumiere, he looked over his shoulder to wave to Sergei, but Sergei was gone.

He must have been lucky and caught a cab right away.

Bob found the restaurant to be charming. Seated near the unlighted fireplace in the center of the room at a table for two, he looked around the filled room at the other diners. He saw Helen Thomas, White House news correspondent for at least thirty years. At a table in the back corner he recognized David McCullough. Bob had just finished reading McCullough's "Truman", and thought it was a masterfully written account of Truman's life. He toyed with the idea of telling McCullough how much he admired his writing, but just then the waiter brought him a menu and asked if he would like to order a glass of wine.

As Bob waited for his wine, he looked over the menu. He decided on the entree du jour, Cassoulet Toulousain. Too bad Sergei couldn't have joined him. He didn't like to eat alone. But, then again, maybe it was better to be alone because he was feeling a bit flushed and his skin was damp. Attributing the symptoms to the heat, he picked up his glass of Pouilly Fuisse. He picked up his glass and noticed his hand was trembling. When he took his first sip he felt his muscles relax and his vision blur. He reached for his napkin to blot his face and his glass slid from his hand breaking into shards on the old stone floor.

Bob's waiter, Carlos, ran to the table as diners turned in time to see Bob Hathaway slump to the floor and land beside his broken wine glass. Genevieve, the maître d', rushed over. She asked Bob's waiter what had happened and knelt down and put her hand on his chest and her fingers on his carotid artery on the side of his neck.

"Call 911!" she screamed. She told the waiter to stay with the man on the floor. Bruno, her second in command, attended to the other diners who were either loudly demanding their checks or threatening to leave without paying at all.

Genevieve watched with anxiety as the diners disappeared into the night and the wait staff ran to the kitchen. She returned to stand with Carlos, realizing that ten minutes ago every table had been full. Now there were now only three people in the dining room and one of them was dead.

CHAPTER 12

Dash Santorelli, Washington, D.C., MPD Detective, and the EMTs arrived at La Chaumiere almost simultaneously. A miracle of the first order in Dash's experience. The EMTs went straight to the body and felt for a carotid pulse. He shook his head and said, "He's gone."

The question for Dash was whether the death was natural, accidental, suicide, or homicide. He knew the ME, so that question should be answered soon.

After he pulled on rubber gloves, he reached into the back pocket of the man's pants and removed a wallet. Jotting down the man's name and address he directed the EMTs to take the body to the morgue. Dash asked who was in charge in the restaurant. Genevieve stepped forward and told him that she was the maître d'. When she was asked where the diners were, she told him about the mass exodus after the patron had fallen to the floor and had not gotten up. None of the other patrons wanted to be involved, it seemed, or to try to help.

Dash was left with only the employees to question. There had been five waiters on duty that night, along with Genevieve and the bartender. Genevieve remembered greeting Mr. Hathaway and showing him to his table. Unfortunately, the other waiters and the bartender had been so busy that they hadn't noticed the diners at Carlos's tables.

Dash followed the EMTs to the morgue. He watched the gurney go down the long, dank hall to the morgue. The coroner on duty that night was Vince Amato. He greeted Dash with a slap on the back. Vince and Dash had grown up two houses from each other and had been best buddies since they were in first grade. Dash asked how soon Vince could perform the autopsy. Vince said, "Maybe the day after tomorrow. More likely, the day after that." Dash nodded his head, smiled at Vince, and refrained from asking for priority because he knew the ME's office was always swamped.

He headed back to the station and called the number he had gotten from Bob Hathaway's wallet. As he waited for someone to answer the phone, he wondered if the guy had had a heart attack. Thirty-eight seemed awfully young to just keel over.

*   *   *

Molly had just finished tidying up the kitchen after dinner. She always left the hospital late. It seemed each day there were more patients than the hospital could accommodate. They would have to hire at least one more doctor. Molly poured a second glass of wine and settled into her chair, hoping to relax a bit while leafing through the latest Journal of The American Medical Association.

A little after 9:30 the phone rang. She checked the Caller ID and didn't recognize the number. Probably another robo-call. After she finished her wine, she realized how exhausted she really was. She got up to turn off the lights, go upstairs, brush her teeth, and fall into bed. As she walked by the telephone she noticed the message light blinking. Thinking it might be Bob, she pressed the message button and listened to a man who said he was Donato Santorelli, a Washington, D.C., police detective. He left a number and asked that she return his call at her earliest convenience.

Molly's heart began to race. Her fingers trembled as she dialed the number. Bob was in Washington. Had he been in an accident? A voice from the phone broke her panicked train of thought. She heard a man say that he was Detective Santorelli. "Did you know a Bob Hathaway?"

"He's my husband. What's happened?"

"I'm sorry to have to tell you this, but your husband collapsed in a restaurant in Georgetown and was pronounced dead at the scene. Because the cause of death is unknown, an autopsy will be performed in the next few days." He offered her his condolences and asked if she could come to D.C. to identify the body. He told her that he would pick her up at the airport when she arrived if she would let him know the details of her flight.

After Molly hung up, she slumped into a chair at the kitchen table and began to sob.

It can't be, she thought. It can't be Bob. I have to get to D.C. as soon as possible. She called and made a reservation for the following morning. She called the hospital to say she would be out of town due to a family emergency. Then she packed a bag and, out of habit, set her alarm. However, she didn't sleep a wink. She spent the long night crying.

The following morning Molly walked off the plane with a throng of passengers. At the end of security saw a tall dark-haired man standing with a sign that read Hathaway. Her heart dropped. Dash introduced himself, picked up her suitcase, and led her to his car parked at the curb in front of the airport behind the taxi line.

There was little conversation on the way to the morgue. Until the body was conclusively identified, there was really nothing to discuss. Dash parked his unmarked car in a space at the morgue reserved for police.

While Molly stared ahead in a daze, Dash walked around the car and opened Molly's door. She paused, and then with a look of determination got out of the car. He took her elbow. She welcomed the touch because all she could feel was a mixture of fear and hope. Fear that the body would be Bob. Hope that it wouldn't be Bob.

Molly walked down the forbidding hall to a door with a four by eight foot window covered by a drab muslin curtain. Dash asked Molly to sit on the bench across from the window for a minute while he spoke with the coroner. When Dash returned he sat down beside her. He inquired if she was ready. After a five second pause, Molly lowered her head and nodded slightly. Dash stood and helped Molly rise, taking her by her elbow to walk to the window. He pushed a button at the side of the window and Molly heard a chime ring. The curtains slowly were drawn back and Molly looked at a body covered with a sheet on a gurney. Molly looked straight ahead.

"I'm ready," she nodded her head as if to confirm she was ready.

Dash nodded to the attendant who slowly drew the sheet down from the head of the body. Molly grabbed hold of the window sill and uttered a string of "no's", first in a whisper and then gradually increasing to a shriek. Molly gasped and turned her back to the window, tears falling down her cheeks.

Dash signaled the attendant to close the drapes. He put his hands on her shoulders to steady her and looked at her. She nodded just once, signifying that it was Bob.

Dash tried to steer Molly to the bench before she lost her balance. She shrugged him off and started walking away. The hallway seemed even longer than it had when they had entered only fifteen minutes ago. Once outside, Molly leaned against the building, her tear-stained face turned to the sky.

Dash drove her to The Georgetown Suites on 29th Street, half a block from the corner where Sergei Romanoff and Molly's husband had said goodbye only twenty-four hours before. Dash arranged to pick Molly up in the morning for her flight home.

When Dash dropped Molly off at the airport, he told her once the autopsy was performed, Bob's body could be released. Molly thanked him and asked if he would send a copy of the autopsy to her. He replied that he would and gave her his card, telling her to call him with any questions.

CHAPTER 13

The autopsy report arrived six days later, on a Monday. Monday was the most hectic of days at the hospital. Molly came home after 8 PM and picked up the mail and tossed it on the kitchen table. She had been eating little and put a can of soup on the stove to simmer while she read through the mail, hoping to take her mind away from Bob's death. The first envelope she picked up was from the Coroner of Washington, D.C. She put a hand to her heart and sat still. Then, she turned off the burner under the soup, poured a glass of wine and sat down.

Bob's height had been five foot eight, his weight 170 pounds. The weight of all of his organs was given. All of his organs were normal. No drugs in his blood. He had not had a heart attack! The only anomaly was a minuscule puncture wound on the back of his left thigh.

She still had plans to make for his memorial service on Saturday morning. Bob had expressed his desire for cremation, but his body had not been released yet. Molly decided to go ahead with a small service, inviting only their closest friends for a gathering to remember Bob and his importance to them. The cremation would be done later. Neither she nor Bob had any living relatives. Thus, the assemblage would include only the Petroffs, several friends from Molly's hospital and medical school days, and some of the people who worked with Bob at Petroff Entreprises, Sandra, Les Mazza, and Bob's secretary.

Tommy led off the tributes to Bob, telling everyone that Bob was a key part of Petroff Enterprises' success and that he was like the brother that he had never had. Tommy said he would always miss Bob. Bob's secretary spoke of his kindness to her, his attention to detail, and his integrity. Tears shone in her eyes. Molly's friends from the hospital and medical school had little to add.

On Monday, following the memorial service for Bob, Molly called Dash and asked if she could come to D.C. and talk to the coroner. Dash agreed and made an appointment with Vince.

When Molly arrived and was introduced to Vince, she asked how something that looked like a mosquito bite could be on her husband's thigh when he had been wearing a shirt and a suit. A mosquito in the fitness center? Unlikely. A mosquito in the hotel room? Not likely.

Molly had done her homework and asked Vince Amato why he had only done a simple toxicology screen. It hadn't shown anything out of the normal. Molly wanted an advanced toxicology screen. When she was told that there was no money in the budget, she told Vince that she would pay for it. There had to be an explanation for that mark on Bob's thigh.

* * *

Lars Larson was sitting at his desk in Duluth reading the New York Times. It was only the beginning

65

of May, but already Lars could see the fog rising off Lake Superior as the frozen lake continued to melt. On the third page of the business section he saw a short article with a headline that read:

YOUNG EXECUTIVE'S DEATH REMAINS A MYSTERY

Lars was shocked when he learned that the young executive was Bob Hathaway with whom he had had dinner only a couple of months ago. He put down the paper and called Molly. When she answered he asked, "Molly, this is Lars Larson. I just heard about Bob. What happened?"

"Oh, Lars. Thanks for calling. Bob collapsed on a business trip to D.C. No one can tell me what caused his death. It's all so very strange. He was in perfect health. He didn't smoke. Oh sure he drank but they say he wasn't intoxicated. That couldn't have been the cause. I miss him so much.

"We had a memorial service last Saturday. I'm sorry I didn't get in touch with you."

"Molly, I'm so sorry. Bob and I had dinner just a couple of months ago and he seemed fine. He was a little concerned with his new job, but that's natural. If there is anything I can do, just let me know."

GREENWICH, CONNECTICUT

TUESDAY, MAY 12, 1992

L aura was already lying in bed when Tommy came home. He fixed himself a drink and climbed the stairs to their bedroom. The room was dark and he stole quietly to the bathroom. When he came out the lights were on. Laura was sitting up in one of the upholstered chairs sipping the drink he had set on the table before entering the bathroom.

"Oh," he said "I didn't know you were still awake."

She said "What kept you so long? Were you at the office all day?" He shrugged and reclaimed his drink.

"Make me my own." she said.

Without saying anything Tommy walked down the stairs to the bar and fixed Laura her own drink. When he turned to start back to the bedroom he found Laura standing behind him.

"What's going on Tommy? You've been on edge ever since Bob died."

"It's nothing." said Tommy.

"No. I know you. We've been married for twelve years and I have never seen you act like this. Is it the company? Are you having another affair? What is it?"

Tommy gave Laura her drink and they walked into the library and sat down on the leather couch.

"No, I'm not having an affair. If you must know, before he died Bob questioned some of my business decisions."

"What kind of business decisions?" asked Laura.

"Well, he thought there might be some legal problems with our business plan. I told him he was wrong. I told him he just didn't know how our company worked. I asked him not to pursue the matter. Nonetheless, he persisted. He even mentioned it to Sandra. She told him to forget about it. But he wouldn't stop. Finally I asked Les to see if he could persuade him to mind his own business."

Laura said, "Les! That goon you call a security director? What did he do?" Having an epiphany, Laura shouted, "Did he have something to do with Bob's death? Oh, Tommy what have you done?"

CHAPTER 14

NORWALK, CONNECTICUT

TUESDAY, JULY 14, 1992

Molly stopped her car at the mailbox, pulled out a stack of journals and junk mail, and threw them into the bag of groceries on the seat beside her. As she drove into the garage she wondered where she had put that policeman's business card. Maybe she should give him a call. She still hadn't received the report on the toxicology screen she had insisted be run and for which she had paid $4,500.

She unlocked the door and was greeted by her new housemate, Stella. She looked around to see what Stella had eaten today. Yesterday, the check she had written for the housekeeper had disappeared. The day before, her electric toothbrush had bitten the dust. "Now, you won't be alone," her well-meaning co-workers had told her. They were certain that Stella was the perfect birthday gift for her. They thought she was feeling lost and bereft after Bob's death.

Molly let Stella out the door to the back yard and set about unloading her groceries. She tossed the mail on the kitchen table and put the groceries away. Funny, Molly thought, as she watched Stella chase a squirrel around a tree, "I miss Bob's physical presence, but I don't miss him." said Molly out loud.

She had married later than most of her friends. Bob was a year older and even though they had been married for three years, she still thought of him as a housemate. More a good friend than a husband or lover. He was polite, neat, carried out the trash, and remembered their anniversary and her birthday. Professionally, he seemed to work hard, but never was seen as a success or a leader. He was a good, solid follower of directions. Molly frowned at her thoughts and felt a twinge of guilt.

She let Stella into the kitchen and rinsed and filled her water bowl. After she had put two scoops of dog food in the other bowl, she poured herself a glass of wine and went to her desk to look for the D.C. policeman's business card. She hoped that he was in and that he could help her. As she read the telephone number, she noticed that his name was Donato Santorelli. When she was in Washington he had told her to call him Dash.

It had been a little over two months since she had last spoken with him in Washington, D. C. and ordered the advanced toxicology screen. The phone rang and rang. Molly prepared to leave a message. Then a deep voice with a bit of a rasp said "Santorelli."

After identifying herself, she asked him if the results of the toxicology screen had been returned. Dash told her that he hadn't heard anything, but would check with the coroner and get back to her.

Molly let Stella out in the back yard and carried her wine to the teak table on the deck. She stared into the distance and sipped her wine while Stella once again valiantly attempted to catch a squirrel. Bob is really gone, she thought. Other than Stella there was no one to talk with, go to dinner with, no one to pick up at the train station. No one to tell her about his day. She felt lonely.

Her thoughts were interrupted by the ring of the kitchen phone. It was the Detective. He told her the Coroner had received the results a few days ago, but had been swamped with work. According to Dr. Amato, the results showed nothing new. Molly thanked him and asked that a copy be sent to her.

She placed a wedge of cheddar and a few crackers on a plate and rejoined Stella on the deck. On the weekends, she and Bob used to sit on the deck just like this, cheese, crackers, a glass of Frascati for her and Knob Creek on the rocks for him. She had worked long hours ever since she graduated and as a consequence the only friends she had were the people she worked with. Like Bob. Except Bob seemed to have known Laura Petroff. Hmmm. What a piece of work she was.

I wonder if Bob really met her on the train. Oh, well. No sense in looking for something sinister now. Bob is gone.

* * *

The following week, while Molly was eating lunch in the hospital's staff room, Anne Blynn, the head of the surgery joined her. They both commiserated about the heavy caseloads everyone at the hospital had and tossed around ideas on how to obtain more funding.

"Could I ask you a question Molly?"

71

"Certainly."

"I don't mean to be intrusive but I've been wondering if everything is alright with you. Are you adjusting? You seem distracted."

Molly sat speechlessly for almost a minute. Just as Ann began to apologize for intruding, Molly answered, "I don't know."

That evening she decided to treat herself to dinner at the Roger Sherman Inn in New Canaan. She and Bob had always been frugal because medical school had cost so much. She had almost decided not to splurge, but then remembered Bob had paid off all of their medical school and law school loans by exercising some of the stock options he had received when he became General Counsel of Petroff Enterprises. She decided as she sipped her Pouilly Fuisse, that maybe it was time to figure out the answer to the question Ann had posed to her. Is everything alright?

After a wonderful dinner, Molly drove home and changed into her pajamas and robe. She put her favorite CD on, "Tallis Scholars Sing Palestrina" and curled up on the sofa. She picked up the newspaper and leafed through it, not really absorbing any news, until she saw a large picture of Laura Petroff. Laura had hosted a gala for a visiting artist and Greenwich's A list was in full attendance. What a shallow woman, she thought. Her life consisted of spas, couture clothes, and that Harry Winston rock that she waved under everyone's nose. Molly tossed the paper down.

This house reminded her of Bob. The picture of that vixen in the newspaper reminded her of Bob. The only friends she had were her co-workers and Stella. Just then she realized that she knew the answer to the question Anne had asked her. I'm not alright. I'm not happy.

SAVANNAH, GEORGIA

SATURDAY, DECEMBER 5, 1992

Only two more moving boxes to unload and Molly could relax in her new nest. She couldn't believe that she was really here. The decision to move to Savannah had been a no-brainer. She had almost thrown the brochure out with the other junk mail, but the beautiful picture of a sunset reflecting on water caught her eye. As she leafed through it to look at more pictures showing palm trees and huge, old-looking trees draped with moss, she saw an offer of a free three-day stay.

She knew it was a come-on, an enticement to buy property or a house. Well, they couldn't force her to buy anything, could they?

Accepting that offer was the first big decision she had made as a widow and, boy, was she glad she had. She loved her new home and thanks to Bob's insurance policy, she was able to purchase it outright. She loved the above-average temperature of sixty-six degrees and no snow. A part-time job at Memorial Hospital covered her living expenses, and Stella's. She met new friends through The Village Library, work, neighbors, and a book club. Life is good, she thought.

CHAPTER 15

NEW YORK CITY

THURSDAY, APRIL 21, 1994

After closing on the loan, Tommy and Sandra Cummings traveled to China several times. They met with several manufacturers before selecting one. Production of the DVD players was not moving as fast as Tommy had hoped. There were problems with suppliers of parts and with the design. The original design infringed a patent held by a Japanese company, so the design had to be reworked.

Tommy met with Sandra on Thursday. They discussed the financial condition of Petroff Enterprises. Its condition was becoming perilous. The DVD project was costing money and not generating any. There wasn't enough new investment income coming in. They were having a hard time paying the promised returns for early investors. Not surprising, considering most of the cash was being diverted to Tommy's bank accounts in the Cayman Islands. He and Sandra had decided that it was only a matter of time before the creditors would be banging on the door.

They planned the itinerary for their trip to China the following week. They were going to inspect the plant of the manufacturer they had chosen. Everything was in order.

But, I can't forget that goddamn statue. I've got to find it. Where the hell could she have put it? The statue was nowhere in sight as he packed for the trip.

The limo dropped Tommy, Sandra Cummings and Les Mazza at JFK Terminal One at 2 o'clock in the afternoon. They checked their luggage at the Air China desk and went to the First Class lounge to wait for their flight to be called. "Is this your first visit to China?" Sandra asked Les. Like she didn't already know. Just being polite.

"Yeah. I don't know how you guys can stand a nineteen hour flight every couple of months. How do you do to keep from going crazy?"

"I read. I'll get ready for the meeting with Zhang Wei on Friday. Remember we arrive tomorrow, Wednesday, and we will need some time to get rid of our jet lag." said Sandra.

"What about you, boss?" asked Les.

"I'll do some reading, throw down some stiff liquor, take some pills and fall asleep."

They boarded their plane at 3:30 PM. Thirteen hours later their plane began its descent into the Beijing Capital Airport. It was 6:20 PM local time on Wednesday. Tommy had jet lag. He knew it was about five o'clock in the morning New York time.

"When we get off, let's go to the China Air courtesy lounge. We can take a shower there and maybe that will help with the time change and my hangover. We've got about a two and a half hour layover before our flight to Shenzhen." said Tommy. While Sandra made her way toward the women's shower, Tommy asked Les, "Did you have any trouble getting the documents?"

"No problem boss. This guy I know in Brooklyn does great work, but he's expensive."

"Money's not a concern. As long as he can keep his mouth shut. I'm just worried about everything going according to schedule. A lot depends on it. I wired half of the money to your offshore account. When we get where we are going I'll wire the other half and you'll be set for life." said Tommy.

SHENZHEN, CHINA

WEDNESDAY, APRIL 26, 1994

Somewhat refreshed, the threesome headed for their connecting flight. The flight was crowded and noisy, but it was smooth. The weather was clear until they got close to Shenzhen. Despite no clouds, there was a layer of dark pollution that hung over the city.

"I don't think LA ever had as much smog as this place." said Tommy.

Upon arrival they collected their bags and made their way toward customs and immigration. It took almost an hour to clear. Most of the arriving passengers took the bus into the city, so they didn't have to wait long for a taxi. The ride to the Ritz-Carlton in the Futian district took twenty minutes.

Almost everywhere they looked there were cranes constructing new high-rise office towers and hotels. The city was booming. They checked into their rooms which were located on the eighteenth floor of the hotel.

Tommy said as they reached their rooms, "It's too late to have dinner at a restaurant, so everyone order room service tonight. Tomorrow we can spend the day wandering around the Futian district, do some shopping and we'll plan to have dinner together tomorrow evening after we get rid of our jet lag. I know a wonderful place called Paletto. It's an Italian restaurant right here in the hotel. I've never had a bad meal there. Plan to meet there tomorrow at six." Tommy disliked being a tour guide but on this trip it was entirely necessary. He didn't want his companions to be uncomfortable.

When Tommy got to his room he ordered sandwiches and some champagne. He had the order sent to Sandra's room. He put on a robe and walked down the hall and knocked on Sandra's door. She opened the door, put her arms around him and pulled him into her room.

After tasting the room service food and finishing the champagne, Sandra began undressing in front of the window overlooking the lights of the city. Sandra helped Tommy out of his robe and into the king-size bed.

They spent most of the next day shopping and exploring the Futian district near their hotel. They walked around the Citic City Plaza, an enormous six floor shopping center featuring high end merchandise and jewelry stores. Later they strolled through Lychee Park where they watched photographers taking wedding pictures against alluring backgrounds. Locals took pictures of themselves standing in front of a massive poster of Deng Xiao Ping.

A little after 6 PM, Tommy got off the elevator on the second floor of the Ritz and found Les and Sandra waiting at the entrance to the restaurant. After they were seated, Tommy and Sandra ordered wine and Les ordered a beer. Tommy ordered Black tagliolini "Mondello style", baby squid, sea urchin and ricotta.

Sandra ordered Pesto risotto with Langoustine.

Les ordered Wagyu beef tenderloin, potato puree and tomato marmalade.

They each ordered Tiramisu for dessert. By the time they finished it was nearly 10 o'clock and they said good night to each other. The perfumed air of the hotel wafted after them as they made their way to their rooms.

The next morning Les called the concierge. He told her the rental car he had reserved in his name was going to have to be changed to Tommy Petroff.

"I was supposed to drive Mr. Petroff and Ms. Cummings to You Cao Peng, but I am ill and Mr. Petroff will have to do the driving." He asked the concierge if she could call Mr. Petroff and tell him of the change in plans.

"Do you need a doctor, sir?"

"No. No thank you. Just some rest. Please hold my calls." Les coughed into the phone for effect.

The concierge called Tommy's room and explained that Mr. Mazza was ill and he could not drive them, but that there would be a rental car in front of the hotel at 10. Tommy gave her the address of Zhang Wei's factory in You Cao Peng and asked for directions.

The concierge directed him: "Take S360 east out of town and turn right onto S359 near Baishigang. In about fifteen kilometers, take a right toward Xiashacun. That road will take you to the shore of Mirs Bay. Follow the shore south about another ten kilometers. Be careful on this road. It climbs up the side of the mountain along the cliffs above the bay. It very dangerous."

Tommy and Sandra had no trouble finding the factory. Zhang Wei gave them a tour as well as several samples of the DVD players he was making for Petroff Enterprises. Later they all went to lunch.

By late afternoon they had finished their business. They thanked Zhang and started back to the hotel along the cliff road. There was virtually no traffic so Tommy suggested that they stop and watch the sun set over the bay.

The brilliance of the setting red sun was muted by the smog that covered Shenzhen in the distance. They watched sail boats returning to port. Waves crashed onto the rocks below the cliff.

While they were parked, another car came toward them. As it neared they could see Les Mazza was driving. He slowed and made a U- turn, pulling up behind Tommy's car.

"Keep the car running and put it in drive" said Les as he got out of his rental. "Put the emergency brake on and stand over there. Leave your briefcases and the samples in your car. Power the windows down."

Les walked over to Tommy's car and turned the steering wheel so that the car pointed across the road toward the bay far below. Les got back in his car and slowly pulled forward until his front bumper touched the rear bumper of Tommy's car. He applied power. His car began pushing Tommy's car, slowly at first because the brake was on. He gradually stomped on the gas. The tires on Tommy's car started skidding across the road. Les kept his foot on the gas as Tommy's car bumped over the curb, plowed through some shrubs and went over the cliff. It dropped about 100 meters onto the rocks and then tumbled into the bay. Les got out of the car and looked down. All he could see was the top of the car in the water as it sank.

Tommy and Sandra got in Les's car and he drove them to the Shenzhen Wan Port. He gave them the documents he had obtained in Brooklyn.

Tommy and Sandra caught a bus for the Hong Kong International airport. It took about an hour.

The border guard inspected Tommy's passport, glared at Tommy and looked again at his passport. After a pause, he stamped the passport and motioned him on.

Good job Les, thought Tommy.

He watched Sandra attempt to flirt with the guard who ignored her and cleared her.

Les returned his car to Avis and took a taxi back to his hotel.

The next morning, Les called the front desk to inquire about Tommy and Sandra. They told him that no one had seen either of them.

Les called the US Consulate and told them that Tommy and Sandra were not at the hotel and that he had not heard from them since the morning before. The Consulate contacted the local police who came to the hotel and questioned Les.

"I was supposed to drive Tommy and Sandra to the factory owned by Zhang Wei in You Cao Peng but I became ill and Tommy drove."

The police finally tracked down Zhang Wei. He told them that Mr. Petroff and Ms. Cummings had shown up as expected and left around 6 o'clock. The police checked the local hospitals but no one fitting their description had been admitted. Les called Laura and told her that Tommy and Sandra were missing. Laura called Joe Yang, a good friend, who was the US Trade representative in China. His wife answered and told Laura Joe was in China. Mrs. Yang assured Laura she would have Joe call her as soon as she spoke with him.

CHAPTER 16

GREENWICH, CONNECTICUT

SUNDAY, APRIL 30, 1994

At 10 PM Laura received a call from Joe Yang. Joe told her not to worry. He said he had many contacts with the Chinese government and the US State Department and would try to find out what was happening. Laura said she wanted to go to China as soon as she could but Joe said to wait a few days. He said, "I'll contact the police and the US Consulate on Monday and let you know what I learn."

The next day Joe learned the police had found skid marks on the road Tommy was thought to have traveled. They also found a car in the bay and were in the process of pulling it up the cliff. Later they identified the car as the car rented by Tommy. They found Tommy's briefcase with his passport, Sandra's handbag, briefcase and passport and a woman's high healed shoe in the car but no sign of the bodies.

Joe called Laura and gave her the bad news. "I'll catch the next plane for Shenzhen."

Laura arrived Wednesday. "The police are still searching the bay for bodies Laura, but due to the tides and unpredictable currents they are not hopeful . . ."

After two weeks, the police gave up the search. Joe told Laura that in situations like this the US Consulate could prepare a Report of Death of an American Citizen Abroad. While it was not the same as a death certificate, it would assist the next-of-kin with legal matters that may arise as the result of death. The next day Laura picked up the papers from the consulate and returned to the United States without further ado.

AUSTRALIA

MONDAY, MAY 1, 1994

Hong Kong to Kingsford-Smith airport took ten hours. Despite the ten hour flight in first class with sleeping accommodations, Sandra looked only slightly ruffled. Her eyes were red and scratchy, but expertly made up. Her red hair caught easily back in a ponytail with a glittery scrunchie that belied her sophistication. At five foot ten inches, dressed in a Chanel suit, she swept a path which turned most male eyes between the ages of puberty and senility.

She might have taken the flight well but Tommy did not. He was definitely exhausted. He'd drunk too much Veuve Clicquot and night-capped a few stiff bourbons with a stewardess based out of Hong Kong.

They'd flown Cathay Air to Sydney. Their forged passports proved themselves worthy of their exorbitant cost, but it still took hours to get through immigration and customs.

Customs had gone through their suitcases like white on rice after which Sandra hired a lanky, well-bodied blonde Aussie guy to load their luggage onto a buggy . . . which had since managed to disappear. He'd said his name was "Blue" and he'd get their stuff to the limo. Tommy hustled Sandra out of the terminal to the limo.

"My luggage is not here, Tommy. Those are Gucci suitcases and I have my entire goddamn wardrobe in them. This sucks, I hate this country already. They're like twenty years behind the times here. Can't you do something? . . . anything!!!" Sandra put her mouth in a thin, straight line, abruptly turning it into a reluctant phony smile right at Tommy. "This is not my choice of countries in which to disappear."

Tommy didn't bother to answer her. He had an appointment with a very notable plastic surgeon in an off-region of Queensland, above the Tropic of Capricorn. The clinic was nestled off the beach-strewn coast of Queensland, a dolphin's leap from the Great Barrier Reef.

"Kaye . . . you can buy more . . ." he hissed, already thinking he'd made a mistake. "Please just remember we're Jock and Kaye MacInty now. Alright . . . Kaye??" Heavy emphasis on her new name. He ran fingers through his hair. It felt grimy, oily and a bit thin on top. But, that could be just his imagination. That stewardess didn't seem to mind his hair when they were alone in the galley at 3 AM. Of course, he had given her five Benjies for her time.

"Fine, Jock!" snapped Sandra trying to remember she was Kaye.

Once he'd mollified Kaye with the prospect of more high-end shopping, he helped her into the limo.

"How are yah, Mr. MacInty? Name's Jonesy and just so you know, Blue and me put all your luggage in the boot." At which point he rolled up the dividing screen between driver and passengers and merged into the chaotic Sydney traffic.

Left side of the road driving had always flummoxed Tommy/Jock and he was glad he'd now have the money not to drive until he was good and ready. Eventually he would have to learn since he had to get a driver's license, but that could wait until all the drama had died down.

CHAPTER 17

NEW YORK CITY

THURSDAY, MAY 19, 1994

The trouble started when the Wall Street Journal printed an article about the disappearance and presumed deaths of the CEO and CFO of Petroff Enterprises.

Saul Goldsmith, Executive Vice President of Colonial American Bank called his law firm, Wormslow & Simpson LLP, and spoke to Bradley Morrison, III. "I just heard that Tommy Petroff and his CFO were killed in an accident in China earlier this month. We need to find out who is running the company now. They still owe us almost $400,000,000 including unpaid interest. Your firm put this deal together and I expect you to find out what is going on. We can't afford to take a loss on a loan this large."

"Don't worry, Saul. I'll look into it for you." said Bradley. But Bradley was not the kind of person who put everything else aside to focus on this new project. It took him four days before he was able to find someone at Petroff Enterprises who could tell him anything official. By then, other creditors were way ahead of the bank in getting information. The information was bad news.

Petroff Enterprises was delinquent on many of its loans and its obligations to investors. Bradley called Saul back and said, "It seems your loan is not the only one Petroff is delinquent on. It hasn't paid its obligations to investors either. Most of these other loans are unsecured and of course the investors have no collateral. You still have collateral in the warehouse subsidiary, TP Logistics, and the inventory in the warehouses. My advice is for the bank to throw Petroff into bankruptcy. If we move quickly before the company loses any more money, we might be able to have the warehouses and the inventory sold, and salvage something."

"Do it and do it fast." said Saul. Bradley filed a bankruptcy petition the next week and a receiver was appointed by the court. The receiver eventually discovered much to the disappointment of the creditors, Petroff Enterprises had no cash and all of its assets were pledged as collateral for loans. That meant that the investors and a majority of the creditors would receive zip, nada, zilch. They were screwed.

As far as the secured creditors, including Colonial American Bank, they might receive some dividend but it might be as little as twelve cents on the dollar.

The warehouses were not assets because they were leased. The inventories were far less than anticipated. Petroff had been falsifying orders and shipping documents so that it appeared that there were substantial inventories, when in fact there was hardly any inventory at all. The only bright spot was that the company had purchased a life insurance policy on Tommy Petroff. It had a $5,000,000, value and it would be available to the creditors unless the insurance company balked at paying without Tommy's body being found.

The creditors filed a civil suit against Laura Petroff. Her assets included her jewelry; the Treetops mansion; the proceeds of another life insurance policy on Tommy; and her shares of stock in Petroff Enterprises. But the creditors were unable to prove that the jewelry, the house or the insurance premiums had been paid for by the company. In the end, they couldn't touch her personal assets. All that was available for the creditors were her Petroff Enterprises shares which were worthless.

The creditors filed suit against the insurance company that issued the life insurance policy on Tommy. Eventually, the insurance company accepted the "Report of Death" issued by the US Consulate in Shenzhen, China, in lieu of a death certificate and paid the proceeds of the policy into the bankruptcy court to be divided among the creditors as directed by the court. That provided the creditors with something. It also prevented the insurance company from challenging Laura's claim under the similar life insurance policy issued on Tommy of which she was the sole beneficiary.

The US Attorney for the Southern District of New York instituted a criminal investigation into the activities of Petroff Enterprises. He could not prove that anyone other than Tommy Petroff, and perhaps Sandra Cummings, had anything to do with the fraud perpetrated on the investors and creditors. With Tommy and Sandra both dead, the investigation was closed without any charges being filed.

Petroff Enterprises ceased to exist after the bankruptcy case ended. Its employees were let go without severance. The lenders, creditors and investors lost millions.

The first thing that Saul Goldsmith did when the dust had settled was to call Richard "Stinky" Rosen and fire Wormslow & Simpson as the bank's attorneys. Rosen called Bradley Morrison, III, into his large corner office on the 46th floor. "What the hell happened Morrison?" he demanded.

"I don't know. Bob Hathaway worked on this. He was supposed to make sure the bank's loan was secured by collateral. I guess he screwed up."

"I know what happened. You were supposed to handle the Bank's account. You were too lazy and you farmed it out to a six year associate. This was a $400 million deal! I think that warrants the attention of a partner, even a junior partner. Bob was neither. But you, Morrison, have no worries. You won't have those kinds of responsibilities anymore. You're fired." said Rosen.

The Chairman of the Colonial American Bank met with Saul Goldsmith shortly after noon on Tuesday, May 31st. "Come in Saul. Do you know that because of that Petroff deal we are going to have to amend our government filings? It is not every day that a national bank loses hundreds of millions of dollars on a single deal. What were you thinking? Petroff was a scam. You would have found that out if you had done the usual due diligence." said the Chairman.

"I did my best," said Saul. Our lawyers fumbled the ball. I fired them." said Saul.

"Good." said the Chairman. "Now it's my turn. You're fired or you can retire if that's what you prefer."

"I don't want to retire. I have worked twenty-five years for this bank and I have done a good job."

"Yes, you worked hard. But you really screwed this deal up and you're gone."

"But I'll never get another job. I'm almost fifty-five years old." said Saul.

"Well, then maybe you should move to Florida, buy a trailer and live off your pension. Oh, I forgot. You aren't vested in your pension until you've worked thirty years. Too bad. Have a nice life living off your Social Security when you start collecting it in another seven years. Good luck, Saul."

CHAPTER 18

GREENWICH, CONNECTICUT

TUESDAY, OCTOBER 17, 1995

Who knew? Laura pushed her fork through the Tuna Nicoise salad, trying to avoid the larger pieces of lettuce which wouldn't fit perfectly into her mouth without smudging her lipstick. A few delicate mouthfuls later, she looked over at Javier who was wending his way back from visiting the men's room. A tableful of Greenwich's wealthiest women had stopped him . . . cold. There were at least three women with humungous breasts, off the shelf, threatening to pop out, cleavages breathing in a rhythm that could cause a tectonic plate shift.

She could hear them bantering for his time, complimenting his sculptures, making arrangements to fund his art shows.

"Oh Javier, you know my husband Antonin? He's the CEO at those Pepsico Corporate Headquarters. Well, my dear, he wants three of your pieces for their Sculpture Garden." She smiled, stood and pressed her breasts, loosely encased in Valentino, towards Javier's torso. "Say luncheon on Thursday to discuss details?" She smiled coyly.

"*Si, si, cara mia,*" murmured Javier as he took her hand, turned it over and planted a soft kiss. "We talk later . . ."

Laura couldn't believe it had come to this. She almost swatted her face with an indelicate-sized chunk of lettuce. The Greenwich Country Club shouldn't allow such riff-raff inside their doors and to top it off that woman clearly had an inferior plastic surgeon.

This particular behavior towards Javier had been growing disproportionately since his work had become immensely popular. Laura had always felt herself to be Javier's DeMedici - a patron who supported his work.

"He lives in my artist studio, for crying out loud."

At a big company party Laura had thrown, it turned out she actually had to wrest him away from another woman. What was her name? . . . the wife of that nosy lawyer who'd been . . . laid to rest. Now, what was her name? Mitzi - Madeleine - Maggie - Manstealer – Molly . . . That was it, Molly. She had been a nurse or worked for a doctor or something.

Javier had expressed an entirely inappropriate interest in Molly. So Laura took care of that and they'd been happily in flagrante ever since.

Poor Tommy, she mused. He'd been too controlling for his own good. He should have hired a driver instead of driving himself to those horrible cliffs somewhere in China. Well, c'est la vie.

Laura had originally made a deal to sell the property to a real estate developer who'd wanted to turn the seventy of the acres in Greenwich into five acres plots to build a series of unGreenwich-like mansions. The plans got turned down by the town of Greenwich. Laura did not particularly care if the Treetops property was turned into a Fun Park, a fracking site or a low cost housing project. Finally, in desperation because the mortgage payments were so large, she agreed to sell the mansion and the entire one hundred acres to the Stamford and Greenwich Land Conservation Trusts. After satisfying the mortgage, she deposited four million dollars in her bank account. Her plan included having Javier to herself . . . without having to compete with those petty, conniving Greenwich pseudo-elites for his affections.

With a sigh of satisfaction and a smile, Laura popped a small forkful of fresh tuna into her mouth.

Javier had been traveling down south far too much lately. His pieces were in high demand down in those backwater places like Miami and Jacksonville and Jekyll Island. But she had a plan to take care of that aspect too. She'd remembered this great ad in Town and Country. The article was about a gated community in a completely artsy setting down in Georgia on an island surrounded by marsh and water.

SKIDAWAY ISLAND
A GEORGIA GEM
IN SCINTILLATING SAVANNAH

CHAPTER 19

FITZROY ISLAND, AUSTRALIA

WEDNESDAY, JULY 7, 1994

A bit over one mile squared and essentially the top of a volcano. Fitzroy Island protruded from the ocean after the last Ice Age cut a swath through the valley connecting it to the mainland. Most of the island was National Park, so Jock's clinic sat hidden in palm trees, gum trees and wild tropical foliage on the western side. The surgery had cost Jock a veritable fortune and he had no regrets spending it. The only glitch was Sandra. He would take care of her in time.

The boat ride over from the mainland, a mere forty five minutes had sent his gag reflex into pandemonium despite the overdose of Dramamine.

Exquisite tropical Australian scenery was one thing, but he preferred to view it from the mainland thank you very much. He'd be glad to dump this "living in isolated nature" for living in mainland nature with a pool and a view of the sea from a great distance.

Cairns sunshine trekked down from the atmosphere at a gentle, well-appreciated pace. It was July. Winter above the Tropic of Capricorn. Weather edged at around seventy degrees . . . or 21.111 degrees centigrade. Metric ruled in the Land of Oz.

Sandra had been busy while Jock went under the knife. She'd taken to shopping as soon as she'd won his devotion. Now she'd be in competition with his wife Laura, whom he'd conveniently left, well taken care of, back in Greenwich, Connecticut, in the good old U. S. of A. In fact, Laura was now considered a wealthy widow after his staged fiery car crash off a cliff into bottomless waters in China. However, that seemed like a lifetime ago. And so it was, he was now Jock MacInty and married to Kaye.

His Kaye (well, he did own her . . .) had since bought a property in a ritzy, well-heeled suburb of Cairns on the mainland. Edged with high walls, the property had hectares of tropical foliage and an Olympic-sized swimming pool. The house on the pinnacle of a mountain was covered with every shade of greens interspersed with a variety of pinks, reds, and blues. He really wasn't into all this Mother Nature stuff, but it worked for his present life style.

*   *   *

Here he continued to languish, some six weeks later. He lay on the chaise lounge beside the clinic's pool. His facial bandages had been removed and now he had a slew of steri-strips along his incision lines - brow lift, chin implant, eye shape change, nose job and face lift to top it all off. Jock changed his hair color to brown. His white streak dyed to match the rest.

On the dock of Fitzroy Island, he threw back a handful of Dramamine and watched his private launch zipping towards him. Three people on board. The Captain, yet another of those muscle-bound, bronzed Australian males. Another man of indeterminate age also tanned, in pressed shorts and a pristine, short-sleeved shirt, both hands firmly planted on deck edge. And Kaye, one hand clutching the vessel side and the other clamped to a large sunhat on her head, looked very much a native. Albeit a rich native. Her see-through "throw-over" she wore over her bikini was whipped by the ocean breeze and left little to wonder about.

"Jock, honey. This is Adams." Kaye gushed, grabbing the arm of the man with the shorts and button-up shirt. "He's our new major-domo." Kaye bestowed her most alluring gaze up and down Adams like a laser setting up a target. "I've given him our new pool house to live in because he came with such good references. An English Lord brought him to Australia and when the guy went back, Adams stayed here. He's agreed to run our household and I told him you'd pay handsomely." Kaye smiled serenely.

A little bold, even for Kaye, mused Jock. The guy's old enough to be her father.

"How do?" Jock returned trying not to stretch his new tight facial skin any more than was absolutely necessary. I'm sure we'll get along. Thinking, until you try to filch cash from me then you're out the door quicker than a gnat's fart. Did this country even have gnats?

Jock wanted to keep a low profile in Cairns. On the other hand, Kaye wanted to socialize, throw parties, meet the young go-getters of Cairns, go high-end shopping in Brisbane, perhaps Sydney, she'd mused. However Brisbane was quite provincial. For the first time it occurred to him that he might not have the funds to support his life style . . . and hers.

The parties were lavish - many pool parties - always peopled with youth and designer names. Their private chef designed perfect cuisine for perfect people. Jock had no problems with the party people. He loved all those fresh bodies who were willing . . . Nonetheless, at the rate of return after Kaye's elaborate spending, Jock would need to get back to Connecticut for a financial replenishment.

Kaye was becoming an increasing problem. After a few years, she'd thought herself a true-blue Aussie and she wanted to drive inland.

Who knows what alien monsters lurked away from the semi-civilization of Cairns . . . rain forests, deserts, bush, Cassowaries, dingoes, kangaroos, wallabies, emus, camels.

"Tommy? Sorry." she smiled, "I mean Jock," she was barely out of her hangover from last night's party. Breakfast fare was spread out on a wrought-iron table on the deck overlooking a goodly portion of the city. She scooped up a mango omelet and a glass of freshly squeezed local guava juice. "Let's take a trip over to Kakadu National Park in Northern Territory. Everyone has been there. We could drive in a week. I could get tremendous photos . . . and maybe even go to Darwin for a day or two."

Jock chewed on his steak and eggs. No way was he eating that other lightweight stuff she made their chef do for her. He could tell her to can it but he had been thinking of exploring the region and beyond.

Who knows what he could find. What opportunities would arise.

"We'll take the Range Rover and have Adams pack all my accoutrement," she added. "I'm sick of Cairns."

After a year or so of her extravagant shopping in Sydney, Jock had put a stop to it. She was bleeding money - his money. Unfortunately, nothing was too expensive or impossible.

You'd never know she was a goddamn MBA the way she acted in Cairns.

"Y'know, I think it would be great for both of us. Adams'll take care of the house while we're gone. Alexa can cook him her famous vegan meals. Jock mused and stared off into the leafy background. A plan was hatching somewhere in the back of his animal brain. He stared at the back of Alexa as she exited with empty plates and thought how he'd miss her nightly visits to his room. He'd be down a lot of green backs while holidaying at Kakadu. He and Kaye already had separate suites in their house so there wasn't any overlapping of exposure. He'd been sick to death of Kaye even before they got to Cairns. But right now, to coin a phrase, she knew where all the bodies were buried.

Adams could get their gear together in a heartbeat. The man was almost indispensable. Adams was a truly incorruptible major-domo. He and the chef, Alexa, were the only staff.

After living in Australia for almost thirteen years now, Jock had perfected the art of left side driving. Besides, Kaye hated driving or doing anything for herself when money could buy someone else to do it.

This would be her big debut into the real world. No servants. No pool. No 1000 count sheets to tumble across at nights with that never-ending migraine looming. No hot tub off her balcony. No mango omelets. No Chanel or Valentino. Definitely no perfume because the mosquitoes, big as 747's would carve a landing strip through her body hairs straight to her blood. The thought of that special torture almost made Jock suggest she bring her favorite perfume. So he did.

"Why don't you bring that perfume that I love to smell on you?" Jock whispered in her ear as he passed. Yes, his plan was hatching. "Oh, let's not take our mobile phones. Let's do 'au naturale', no stock markets reports, no texts, no nothin'. Think you can do it Kaye?" He truly wondered if he himself could perform such an odious task.

"Of course I can, I don't need to have a mobile phone grafted to my ear. That's you. Let's see if you can do it." The game was afoot.

CHAPTER 20

Three weeks later they hit the road to Kakadu. Range Rover packed with sleeping bags, extra petrol, water, snacks and assorted foods. 1,308.18 miles. Or, if you wanted kilometers a mere 2,878. Five or six days on the road with reservations at every pub where they were likely to stop. Adams took care of all the bookings, because there was no way Jock was going to camp out on raw territory. Sleeping bags were in case pubs didn't have clean sheets. For a day they traveled up verdant hills smudged with tropical colors with black tar roads.

"God, I hate these endless roads of nothing, Jock." Kaye stared out the window. "Do you think we'll get to Jabiru and that famous Crocodile Hotel by nightfall?"

"Let's just stop near this waterfall and maybe we'll go for a swim." suggested Jock.

"Great idea," she burbled, "I'm like so fed up with this country. One second it's red dirt and nothing, the next long weird grass, snakes, goannas up gumtrees and waterfalls and water everywhere."

The land had evolved into a lush mountainous bush with waterfalls, gumtrees, and excellent dams for swimming or whatever.

Jock pulled over and they both got out and stretched. The heat was intense. He took off his jacket and slung it over a sign that read:

CROCODILES
NO SWIMMING

Kaye threw off her clothes without paying the slightest interest to her surroundings. She scampered up on a fallen gumtree trunk for height above the murky watery depth . . . and dived in.

She came to the surface once, briefly . . . before the croc snagged her and dragged her down . . . after which the prehistoric beast started on his buffet lunch.

What a country, mused Jock with a smirk on his face.

Jock retrieved his jacket from the sign and ambled rather leisurely back to the Rover. He drove at moderate pace back to a town they'd driven through, eight hours down the road, Daly Waters - Population 25 . . . a Petrol Station and a pub. Before he got out of the Rover, he took a deep breath and started to hyperventilate and snort. Then he went into the pub and babbled to the bar man.

"Where's the nearest Police station? Please help me. I think my wife drowned. She disappeared after she dived into a murky dam. I think a croc got her because I told her about the sign saying, no swimming - crocodiles, and she poo-pooed me."

The bar man, tattooed with a white singlet and overhanging belly answered, "Well, Matey, it's a good three hours down the road."

*   *   *

Some hikers found her body . . . or what was left of it, a week later. By then Jock was back in Cairns acting out his sorrow and arranging to have the body flown back for burial. It all turned out to be remarkably simple.

He tearfully gave all her clothes and whatnots to Alexa who just as tearfully accepted them asking at the same time as she held a Gucci gown up to her body, ". . . do you think this will fit me, Jock?" Sniff, sniff. "She was a bit larger than me." Smile, smile. "Oh, is this a Harry Winston ring, Jock? I love Harry Winston. He's really big in America." He'd had to buy Kaye that Harry Winston ring like Laura's, to shut her up.

"You can put on a fashion show for me, later on today." Jock muttered thinking he'd better check his finances and try to re-establish his fortune.

Perhaps a quick trip back to Connecticut might be in order in another few weeks.

However . . . man plans, god laughs . . .

* * *

"Jock," crooned Alexa, "there is one other thing . . ."

"Anything, for you my dear," said Jock feeling quite worldly and generous with his words. "Anything at all."

"Well, I know you are suffering a very big loss and grieving from Kaye's . . ." Alexa paused. She couldn't think of the correct word to use in this situation. She didn't want to seem flippant. Nonetheless, this little nugget of gold would really cheer up Jock. ". . . Kaye's um . . . passing, but I have good news." Alexa smiled and postured herself in her most becoming way. "My darling, I know you love me."

"Yes. Yes. What is it Alexa honey?" He watched the curve of her breasts and angled his eyes to follow her shapely body downwards over her bronzed stomach and legs that he called pillars of Australian democracy.

Alexa slid her hands sensuously to her belly with the Harry Winston ring clearly displayed on the ring finger of her left hand. "Jock, we're going to have a baby . . ."

Jock leapt from the bed and almost slipped to the floor as a whirlwind rush of disbelief flooded his every pore. Blood rushed to his face and then just as quickly sluiced down to his feet. "Sorry?" he forced words from his mouth. "Pardon?"

"I'm just so excited", Alexa burbled on happily apparently not noticing Jock's complete and utter shock.

Jock pulled himself together and produced a tight, thin-lipped smile. "Are you sure, honey?"

"Oh, of course. I saw the gynae doctor in Cairns last week while you were away. He told me I'm well along in the family way. And, all our close friends know . . . I sort of let it drop because they know we're together."

Well, hell. He'd have to think about this. No suggesting she have it taken care of because it seemed the whole goddamn world knew but him. The doc back in Greenwich had told him he couldn't have children because his sperm count spiraled into the low numbers and didn't he say something else about the shape of his sperm?. So Jock had gotten used to no children. He'd thought about it when he first married Laura back in Connecticut, but she told him flat out, no kids. And really, he agreed with her then.

"Aren't you thrilled, Jock?" Alexa interrupted his thoughts. "We'll have the sound of little feet running around this house."

After another ten minutes, fake smiling turning into acceptance. Jock thought, Jesus, now I have to go back to wherever that bitch Laura is, because I really need that stash.

" . . . and we're having a girl . . ." Alexa added.

CHAPTER 21

WEDNESDAY, JULY 7, 2005

Kaye had been dead for a little over a year. Right after Kaye died, Alexa wasted no time moving from the servant's quarters to Jock's suite. She intended to replace Kaye in all ways. She even interviewed and hired a new cook.

Jock didn't approve or object. He felt like he was floating in space with no direction, no goal and no future. Sometimes he thought he actually missed Kaye, although he liked screwing Alexa. He knew his life style was something that would have been the envy of most men, but Jock was only forty-five, way too early to retire.

All of his life he had been driven by business deals and making money. Some legal, some not. For the last ten years he hadn't done anything productive. Didn't really need to work because he still had plenty of money socked away overseas in numbered accounts. Maybe he was bored by the lack of action.

After a late breakfast with Alexa, Jock announced, "I'm going to Sydney."

Alexa never had the money to shop in the big city and she was excited. Unfortunately, Jock told her it was a business trip and she couldn't come. She stood up so fast she knocked her chair over and spilled coffee all over the table. As she stormed out of the kitchen Jock yelled "I'll bring you something nice."

It was only a business trip in Jock's mind. Jock didn't have any business in Sydney, but he felt that he needed a change of scenery.

He flew to Sydney and took a suite at the Park Hyatt. Jock left the hotel about noon. The weather was clear and the temperature was in the high sixties, a good temperature for a brisk walk. He intended to stroll around a district called the Rocks. It was the oldest part of Sydney, the place where the first settlers had landed in the late 1700s. He walked along George Street looking in windows of the art stores they passed.

The area originally was home to many sailors, prostitutes and gangs. Over the last fifty years there was a struggle between those who wanted to tear down everything and build something new because the land was so valuable, and the preservationists. The preservationists stepped in and won. Some, but not all, of the old buildings had been preserved, but for a different purpose. Now it is cleaned up for the most part and is filled with tourists, galleries, pubs and souvenir shops. There were many alleys and narrow streets.

After several days of sightseeing he was bored. Back at the hotel he asked the Concierge where he might find some female companionship. The man told him to try a place called The Fiddle. At around ten that evening, Jock ordered a taxi and took a ride to The Fiddle.

He paid the cover charge and headed to the long mahogany bar. The place was dark but not dirty. The bartender served good drinks. Unfortunately, there were no women at the bar. After several bourbons, Jock struck up a conversation with the big guy sitting next to him at the bar.

"Let me introduce myself. I am Ricardo Salvestori. They call me Captain Panama. I come here a lot when I'm in port."

"Oh, are you a captain of a ship? What cruise line?" asked Jock.

"No. No. Not a cruise line, Pal. I captain cargo ships. At least I did until I got tossed a few months ago for running aground near Mud Island in Moreton Bay on my way to Brisbane."

Panama must have weighed about 160 Kilos. He looked to be in his mid-fifty's, had a receding dark hair, bushy eyebrows, large ears, and a nose that looked like it had been broken many times. His shoulders were wide, his neck was as thick as Jock's thigh, and his teeth were nicotine stained. He had at least three chins and fingers like Polish sausages. Jock thought he looked a little like a young Sydney Greenstreet who played 'The Fat Man' in the *Maltese Falcon*.

Captain Panama spoke with a slight Spanish accent, "I live in Sydney and I sail from Australia to the east coast of the United States almost every month. If I'm not on board my ship I'm here at The Fiddle."

Jock shouted a round and they talked for several hours. Jock was fascinated by the tales Panama told. He described some of the ports his ship called on from New Zealand to Columbia, to Savannah, Georgia, and New Jersey.

"My name is Jock MacInty. I live in Cairns and I'm a private investor. I'm in Sydney looking for places to invest money."

The next several nights Jock returned to The Fiddle. Captain Panama sat on the same bar stool every night and they would talk and drink for hours.

Jock wasn't interested in investing but he was learning a lot about the shipping business. It surprised him to learn that sometimes the large container ships took on passengers. Passengers gave up comfort to avoid immigration scrutiny.

Jock enjoyed his time with Captain Panama, but thought he should probably go back to Cairns. He and Panama exchanged email addresses and planned to stay in touch.

Captain Panama said, "I'll be back in port next month. Once the dates are firmed up, I'll shoot you an email. We can get together and I'll take you down to The Cross."

"Is that King's Cross?"

"The one and only."

CHAPTER 22

SYDNEY, AUSTRAILIA

MONDAY, APRIL 17, 2006

Jock surprised Alexa when he told her he had to go back to Sydney on business. She was furious because she thought he would leave her home again. Instead he said they were both going. While he tended to business she could visit her friend Juno who had a nice house in Watson's Bay. He would drop Alexa with her friend and go see his old pal Captain Panama.

"I have to meet an old friend of mine down at Circular Quay. He's in the shipping business. If you like, Alexa, I'll meet you and Juno for dinner at the Regatta in Rose Bay. We can catch a lift down Old South Head Road and be there in no time."

"Oh, Jock. That sounds like a great idea." She was still in shock Jock had agreed to take her with him this time. Last time he didn't even bring her a T-shirt.

She had to call Juno and see if she could stay there so they could party. That fact Juno was the housekeeper and the owners were off in Europe for a six-month stint was so perfect.

All Alexa had to do . . . was shop her arse off. She could buy things for their baby. Alexa was pregnant and expecting the baby in October.

Jock reluctantly gave Alexa his gold American Express card. "Nice to meet you Juno. Sorry, I have to run. I have a meeting. See you at dinner?"

"We'll meet you there."

Jock said goodbye to Alexa and Juno and made his way to the Fiddle.

When he arrived, Jock saw Captain Panama on his usual bar stool. Jock slapped Panama on the back. "Hey there, matey."

"Glad you're able to make it this week. By the way, I'm working for Chu Logistics Worldwide now. I'm here to meet with my boss tonight. He's negotiating to buy some ships and he wants me to check'em out. I figured you might like to meet him. You did say you were interested in investments. Right?"

"I might like to meet him. I'm always looking for new investments," said Jock cautiously.

Just then an Asian man in a very expensive silk suit stepped up to the bar. With a formal bow he said, "Captain Panama. Good to see you again."

"Mr. Chu when can I check out the ships?"

"We no reach agreement yet on price or delivery. It be a while." said Chu.

"Jock, this is Mr. Chu. Mr. Chu, this is Jock MacInty, an old friend of mine . . . and an investor."

Mr. Chu handed Jock his card which read:

Chu Wei
Managing Director
Chu Logistics Worldwide
Offices in Singapore and Sydney

Strange, thought Jock. No phone number. No address.

Just then, Mr. Chu said, "Let me have that card back for a moment."

Jock handed him the card and Mr. Chu wrote his phone and fax numbers on the back and handed it to Jock.

"So you are negotiating to buy a ship," Jock queried.

"Not one. I'm looking at whole fleet. You know all about expansion of Panama Canal? Well, new Canal won't be finished for five years. When finish, new category of ship can make trip. We call them Post Panamax ship. Post Panamax ship almost three times size. Wider. Longer. New ship carry 14,000 container. New Canal. New big ship. Old ship sell cheap."

"I used to run a private investment fund," Jock lied. I sold my business a few years ago and now I'm looking for something new."

"Interesting." commented Mr. Chu. You give me contact information. I send you information," Chu said. "Now I treat you big dinner"

FITZROY ISLAND, AUSTRALIA

TUESDAY, JUNE 19, 2006

Alexa walked into Jock's home office with two cups of coffee. He was staring at his computer concentrating on the screen while scribbling notations and figures on a yellow pad.

"What's up? You look worried."

"Nothing," said Jock. He never shared information about his finances with Alexa.

"Don't give me that. You've been holed up in this room all weekend. Something is up. Do we have money troubles?"

"No, we're fine."

"Ever since our trip to Sydney you seem to be preoccupied. What is going on?" Alexa wouldn't let it go.

"You wouldn't understand."

"Try me."

"If telling you will give me some peace, I'll try to make it as simple as possible so you might be able to understand it a little. I'm thinking of making an investment in Mr. Chu's business venture. He sent me his business plan and it looks promising. I could earn around 20% on my investment. I'm not earning anything now and you've been burning through our resources. Think of my wealth as a pitcher of water. It was full when I moved here. Kaye poured out about a third. You've poured out more so it is half empty and no one is putting more water in the pitcher. And now we have a baby on the way. I can't go on like this."

"All right, tell me about the plan." Alexa stifled a yawn.

"Chu is going to buy a fleet of cargo ships. The ships are old but still serviceable. He'll lease them to shipping companies. The beauty of the deal is that he will be able to get the ships for less than half of what they are worth. The large carriers are dumping them in favor of the new Post Panamax ships that will be able to use the Panama Canal in four or five years after the expansion is finished."

"How much does he want?"

"He wants five million US for each ship. That would buy a 20% interest."

"You have five million dollars?" Alexa gasped.

"I have nearly sixteen million left in offshore accounts which are paying close to zero in interest. I'm thinking of investing at least ten with Chu if his plans look as good as they seem. I have a lot of studying to do before I would make any investment. There are a lot of crooks out there." Jock turned back to his computer. Alexa took the hint and left.

Jock flew to Sydney almost every week during July and August, 2006 meeting with Chu and his bankers each time. Eventually, Jock was satisfied with the deal and he wired ten million dollars to Chu's account. Chu told him that there would be no profits to share until he had acquired twelve ships which had to be retrofitted. Only then could he lease them to shippers. Jock was OK with that.

*   *   *

Grace MacInty was born October 17, 2006.

PART 2

CHAPTER 23

WASHINGTON, D.C.

SUNDAY, JANUARY 3, 2010

The ringing of the phone brought Dash struggling to untangle himself from the blankets. As he picked up his cell phone, the ringing stopped. He scrolled through the recent calls and saw a number with a 912 area code.

Where the hell is that? Just then the message tone chimed. He tapped play and heard "Dash, you old devil. It's Conor. Call me."

Conor Donovan! His ex-partner. He missed Conor who was about ten years his junior. They had been a great team . . . the two "I's". Conor Irish and Dash Italian. He had been Conor's rabbi when Conor joined the force. They had worked together until five or six years ago when Conor moved his family somewhere down south to be nearer his wife's parents. His wife, Meg, had been born in the south and was an only child. Dash also remembered Conor saying he wouldn't miss the D.C. winters.

Conor answered in his usual happy brogue, "Conor Donovan. At your service."

After catching up with what each had been up to since they last saw each other, Conor told Dash the purpose of his call. The SCMPD (Savannah-Chatham Metropolitan Police Department) was looking to hire experienced police officers and found that they were scarce as hen's teeth. "Come on down to Savannah and work with me. We can be the two 'T's' in Savannah".

"You know Conor, I've been thinking of retiring. I've spent thirty six years in the D.C. Police Department. I'm burned out. I'd like to wind down my career and find something with less stress. Maybe find a gated community looking for a Security Chief and enjoy life at a slower pace."

Conor let out a hoot! "Dash, my man, do I have just the spot for you! There's a place up in Hilton Head, SC, that is looking for a Security Chief. They have been calling my partner down here who's right around your age. I know for a fact that he isn't interested because his wife won't move up there, too much traffic. She's a Savannah girl. She'll never leave."

Dash was silent for a few seconds and then said, "Give me the info, Conor. I'm ready for a change."

SAVANNAH, GEORGIA

MONDAY, FEBRUARY 1, 2010

Dash walked out of the plane and into the airport, following the lemmings in front of him. When he passed out of the security area he found himself in a charming, large, square room with rocking chairs, a few tables, benches, and a large four-sided clock hanging from the ceiling in the center of the room. This airport certainly beat the normal sterile airport lounge look. It actually seemed designed for travelers to be comfortable. He had never seen so many smiling faces in any other airport. Vacationers probably.

That evening he had dinner with Conor and his wife Meg at a place downtown, The Olde Pink House. Conor made it clear to Dash that dinner was his treat to welcome him to Savannah and to wish him luck with his interview in the morning at Sea Cove. Dash was impressed with the dinner and noted of the slower pace of southern life.

The following morning he plugged in the address of Sea Cove into his phone and took off over the Talmadge Bridge to South Carolina. Less than an hour later, he pulled up to the gate and gave the Security Office his name. The gate arm rose and he wended his way to Sea Cove's association offices. He was greeted with a smile and immediately ushered into the office of the association's president, Jack Tatum.

Mr. Tatum explained, "This job entails the security of our residents and all property within the gates."

The two talked for another hour and a half. Dash did his best to absorb it all.

Glancing at Dash's CV, the President said, "Masters Criminal Justice from George Washington University . . . Impressive. We don't usually have candidates with this kind of education. Thirty-six years with the D.C. police department. . . . Tell me a little about that."

When Tatum asked Dash if he had any further questions, Dash asked if it would be possible to speak with the current Chief of Security.

Tatum looked uncomfortable. "I'm afraid that isn't possible. You see, we have been without a Chief for six months, due to his sudden death. I've been interviewing non-stop since the Chief's death. We've had no really good prospects . . . but I think you might be one. Could you stay with us a few days? I'd like for you to learn more about the community and meet with our Board of Directors. I'll set up a meeting with them for 1 o'clock tomorrow."

Dash, who rarely smiled, almost smiled.

The community tour proved interesting. Nothing could have been less like D.C. and the weather was blissfully temperate. He had left D.C. in a blizzard and had no desire to return there.

The meeting at 1:00 was stress-free, more like a get together in the break room back at the station. There were ten men and women along with President Tatum.

The questioning was friendly until a Mrs. Bainbridge rose and began her inquisition.

"Mr. Santorelli, will your wife and family be joining you?"

Before Dash could answer, Tatum looked her in the eye and said, "I hardly think Mr. Santorelli's marital status has any bearing on his qualifications."

Still standing and staring straight at Tatum, Mrs. Bainbridge continued. "Have you ever killed anybody?"

"Mrs. Bainbridge. That is enough. Sit down."

After an hour, which was much like the interview with Tatum, he was asked if he minded waiting in the anteroom for a few minutes.

Ten minutes passed. He was invited back into the conference room. Everyone was smiling except Mrs. Bainbridge.

The President stood, leaned over the table, looked at Dash and said, "We have decided to offer you the position of Chief of Security. Since we discussed the salary and benefits yesterday, would you be interested in joining us at Sea Cove?"

Dash rose to his full six feet and looked each person in the eye, including Mrs. Bainbridge. "I am honored. Thank you. I accept your offer of employment."

After he had returned his rental car, he took the shuttle bus to the terminal and saw that he had an hour before takeoff. He pulled out his cell phone and called Conor. No answer. He left a message. "I'm on my way to D.C. to pack. See you soon."

CHAPTER 24

HILTON HEAD, SOUTH CAROLINA

MONDAY, MAY 14, 2012

He was astonished over two years had passed since he had started to work as head of Security for Sea Cove. He'd even survived Mrs. Bainbridge, the terror of Sea Cove. She had scowled when he first met her at his interview. Since then she'd never stopped scowling whenever he was in her presence.

Mrs. Bainbridge called him weekly to complain about anything that irritated her. She drove around Sea Cove and jotted down the house numbers of anyone who put their trash cans out by the street before the appointed time on Monday morning. These house numbers were given to Dash weekly. She gave him the license number of every car that drove two miles over the posted speed limit that had the misfortune to be driving in front of her. Sea Cove was not a large community. Mrs. Bainbridge knew every teenager by name thus allowing her to report every one of them who offended her interpretation of the rules of the community. Mrs. Bainbridge, the bane of his otherwise idyllic existence at Sea Cove, was beginning to wear thin.

Last weekend, Dash joined Conor and Meg for dinner at a backyard barbecue at their home on Isle of

Hope. He found himself complaining to them about Mrs. B as they watched the tide come in.

"Sounds like Mrs. B wants your job, Dash. You're only sixty-two. Why don't you see if there are any other communities looking for someone to head up their security program. There are hundreds of gated communities in South Carolina and Georgia. And you instituted that new computer program that tightened up Sea Cove's security. That was quite a feather in your cap, boyo. You told me it really cut down thefts by keeping unauthorized visitors and vendors out of Sea Cove."

"Well, maybe. I know three things: Mrs. B accounts for fifty percent of my work load; I don't like trying to avoid her; and, I hate complaining about her to you two. Maybe I'll see what's out there."

SAVANNAH, GEORGIA

WEDNESDAY, DECEMBER 5, 2013

He couldn't believe he had landed this job at The Landings. There had been a lot of competition and numerous second and third interviews of each of the many candidates by the Association's Board of Directors. And now Dash was the Chief of Security for a community of 8,500 people, six golf courses, four club houses, a fitness center, a tennis center, and two marinas. This community is three times the size of Sea Cove.

I hope I'm up to it.

The Landings wanted him to put into place the same computerized AXIS security program that he had installed at Sea Cove. He was pretty certain having done the installation at Sea Cove was what gave him the edge over the other candidates. He looked forward to the challenge despite knowing that it would take well over a year to be fully integrated. Dash was confident. After all, this was his second rodeo.

Because of the number of residents and the numbers of service people who entered the gated community each day, there were too many opportunities for theft. The new AXIS program would reduce the numbers of unauthorized people entering and the number of thefts. It had worked that way at Sea Cove. No reason it wouldn't work that way in The Landings.

He purchased the least expensive townhouse in The Landings. He felt it was important to live in the community he was charged with protecting.

His townhouse overlooked a golf course and had a small patio off the kitchen. The new table and chairs, gas barbecue, and two rockers made a pleasant place to eat after his day in the office. While Dash's hours were nine to five Monday through Friday, he was officially on call twenty-four seven as Chief of Security.

Tonight, he decided to grill a steak that he had bought at Smith Brothers. He turned on the grill, opened a bottle of Yuengling and sat down to skim over the latest report from the COO of The Landings Association.

A voice said, "Hi there!"! Dash looked up and to see a man in his fifties wearing a golf shirt and shorts and holding a can of beer. "I'm Carl Riemenschneider. I live next door."

Dash introduced himself and asked Carl to join him.

"I haven't seen your wife. Is she moving in later?"

When Dash explained that he wasn't married, Carl smiled and told Dash that he wasn't married either. "My wife and I divorced several years ago. She moved back to Northern Virginia to be near our daughter, a single mother with three children. Our marriage wasn't bad, it was just that the only thing we had in common was our daughter and our daughter was the only thing that interested Barb. So, when she said she was leaving there was no animosity and we parted friends. Whoa! Barb always told me I talked too much. What about you?"

Shades of Mrs. B.

Dash gave him an abbreviated rundown of his D.C. and Hilton Head jobs. He added he was the newly hired Chief of Security for The Landings Association. "I'm about to throw a steak on the grill. It's big enough for both of us. Let's split it."

As they ate steak and a salad with Dash's special Italian dressing, Carl said "I'm head of IT for the Savannah-Chatham Metropolitan Police Department. I don't suppose you know Conor Donovan?"

"I sure do! He's a great guy."

"How do you know him?"

"We were partners on the D.C. police force. In fact, it was Conor who told me Sea Cove was looking for a Chief of Security. After I got things in order at Sea Cove, the job got a little humdrum. I heard about this job and here I am."

* * *

The next weeks were jam-packed full with meetings with the vendor for the new security program. With a bit of luck, they could start initial installations in March and start seeing a reduction in unauthorized entries and thefts fairly soon.

* * *

A vision of Ellie flashed before him. He wished she could be with him now.

CHAPTER 25

FRIDAY, APRIL 25, 2014

The past four months had flown by. Dash loved his work and was excited to be at the point of the first new security installation. The weather was to be in the mid-eighties over the weekend. Dash called Conor and invited him and Meg to come over to celebrate the end of the first phase of the AXIS program.

I've been so busy I haven't seen Conor in months. In fact, all I seem to do is work and sleep and wave at Carl when we get in our cars in the morning.

They inhaled their dinner of a Spicy Clam Roast to which Dash had added sweet local shrimp. After dinner and a dessert of Blueberry Crisp, Conor, Meg and Dash sat on the patio and sipped the last of the Sangria.

Meg asked Dash for the recipe for the Clam Roast and said in her soft Savannah drawl, "I don't know how a bachelor cop can be a gourmet cook, but you surely are, darlin'."

"My mom was a fantastic cook and she told me I'd better learn or I would starve to death. I like to eat. I learned to cook."

Meg coerced him to write down the list of ingredients so she could try her hand at the dish.

"I don't have a recipe, I just put things together."

Conor groaned, "Enough of this food talk. I'm stuffed. Tell me, Dash, who else have you met around here?"

"Well, there's you and Meg and Carl, next door."

"You can't work all the time. All work and no play, you know? We don't want people callin' you dull, Dash, me boy."

FRIDAY, JUNE 13, 2014

Dash and Carl snagged the last spot in the parking lot and wondered if they would be able to find a table. Carl had talked him into joining him for dinner at Driftaway in nearby Sandfly. The tables on the porch were all filled and a guitarist was playing blue grass and country songs.

"All of the tables inside are filled, but there are two empty seats at the bar," the hostess informed them.

They looked at each other, nodded, and headed for the bar. The noise level was deafening. Typical Friday night. Everyone seemed to be letting off steam from the work week. As Dash looked around the bar he noticed an attractive woman seated on the last stool at the far end of the bar. Just then she looked up and Dash thought to himself, she reminds me of someone.

Carl and Dash ordered and after some conversation about how the installation of the AXIS program was going, Dash asked Carl "Do you know the woman at the end of the bar?"

Carl said "I don't, but I've seen her around town."

Their orders of Tybee Tuna and Sandfly Fish and Chips arrived and they dug in and all talk stopped.

Dash pushed the button to unlock his car and noticed someone standing at the driver's door of the car next to his. It looked as if the person was trying to break into the car. Dash walked around the back the car and saw the woman from the end of the bar. "Can I help you?"

Startled, she turned to him and said "I've locked my keys in my car. Stupid me."

They both stared at each other and began to speak at the same time. "Are you . . . Don't I know . . ."

Then Molly smiled up at him. "I'm Molly Cohen. Where have I seen you before?" Could it be that D.C. detective who helped me when Bob was killed?

"Have you ever been a police detective in Washington, D.C.?"

"Yes, I was. Now I live in The Landings and I am the Chief of Security.

Dash continued, "You seem familiar to me too. Have we met before Molly Cohen?"

The smile left Molly's face as she said, "I can't remember your name, but I believe we met in Washington almost twelve years ago. My husband was on a business trip there and suddenly died. You were kind enough to pick me up at the airport and try to help me understand what happened to him. He was dining at a restaurant in Georgetown and . . . just died. The coroner never found the cause of his death."

"I apologize. My name is Dash Santorelli, and I do remember you now. Didn't you push for a more advanced toxicology screen? Did anything show up?"

"No, nothing. I can't believe you remember me. I can't believe that we are both here in Sandfly, Georgia. How in the world . . . ?"

Dash noticed Carl standing beside him like a bump on a log and proceeded to introduce Molly to Carl. "Be right back," he said as he strode to the trunk of his car.

131

He returned with his Slim Jim and in seconds, Molly's car door was unlocked.

"How can I ever repay you?"

"Maybe you would have dinner with me sometime?"

She pulled out her cell phone and grinned. "What is your cell phone number?"

He told her his number, she swiftly tapped it into her phone. As he watched her grinning up at him, his phone rang. His caller ID showed: Molly Cohen.

"Now you have my number . . . and I have yours. Thanks a million for bailing me out of my self-induced, embarrassing predicament. 'Night, gentlemen!"

Carl ribbed him all the way home. "Lothario, Casanova. Don Juan." Even though the inside of the car was dark, Carl could see Dash's reddening face reflected in the lights of the instrument panel.

CHAPTER 26

FRIDAY, JUNE 27, 2014

He had dated a few women over the past thirty years, but had found none of them to be of interest. He hadn't wanted a relationship anyway, had he? He had been consumed by his work. None of the women had come close to reminding him of Ellie, his first and only love who was taken away from him almost fifty years ago. The picture in his mind of Ellie being dragged into a car by three men still caused his heart to ache. The sound of the squealing tires roared in his head. The car sped off leaving Dash dazed and bleeding on the side walk.

He and Ellie had been walking home after seeing "*Fiddler on The Roof*", their hearts filled with love, as they hummed "If I Were a Rich Man". So long ago.

* * *

He realized thoughts of Molly had crossed his mind almost daily since that night at Driftaway. He waited almost two weeks to ask her to dinner. He didn't want to seem too forward.

He still wasn't interested in a relationship, but everyone has to eat dinner. Maybe Molly would have dinner with him. She gave me her number. But . . . she has mine too. And she hasn't called. Oh, well. Nothing ventured, nothing gained.

He was tired of eating with Carl every other night. On the other hand, Conor and Meg were fun to be with, but it was always a threesome when they got together. Threesomes are always awkward. Maybe he would give Molly a call.

As he picked up his phone to call her, it dawned on him the following Friday would be the Fourth of July. That would make it three weeks since they had exchanged phone numbers. Surely, that was a decent enough interval. She wouldn't think he was chasing her, would she?

If she accepted his offer, maybe Conor and Meg would join them. Meg, always a great talker, put people naturally at ease. If they could join him and Molly, it might make their first evening together less tense. Dash had to admit to himself he was nervous.

When Molly answered, he asked her how her week had been.

"I didn't think you would ever call! I thought you were just being polite."

Taken aback, "I've been busy investigating some vandalism on the golf courses. Do you have any plans for the Fourth of July?"

"No. No plans yet."

"Why don't you come to my house for dinner? I'd like you to meet some friends of mine." He thought he heard a small giggle.

"I'd love to come and meet your friends."

As it turned out, Molly got to meet all of Dash's friends. All three of them.

In the late afternoon on the fourth he had been cleaning the patio and the grill in preparation for dinner when Carl appeared like a jack-in-the-box from around a tall shrub.

"What are you up to, Dash? Do you always have a cleaning frenzy on the Fourth?"

"I'm having friends over for dinner tonight." He looked up at Carl and saw disappointment written on his face.

"OK, see you later. Have fun."

"Carl, if you don't have any plans, would you like to join us?" Carl's face lit up and he said "What time? I'll bring the wine!"

SATURDAY, JULY 5, 2014

Dash awoke to the sound of a Pileated woodpecker hammering away. He glanced at the clock. It's only six. I'm awake now. I might as well get up. Reluctantly, he got out of bed and as he stepped into the shower, he found himself whistling. It almost made him laugh. He couldn't remember if he had ever whistled in his life. Maybe when he was in grade school? He smiled, something he didn't often do, and wondered if his whistling had anything to do with the great fourth of July he had spent with Carl, Conor and Megan and Molly.

The picnic had been perfect. He had borrowed a golf cart for Conner and Megan to use from a neighbor who spent every summer in Minnesota. After supper, he and Molly in one cart, Conor and Megan in the other cart, set off to Deer Creek Golf Course to watch the fireworks. Carl followed them in his own cart. They found perfect spots and parked with Carl in the middle.

There must be a thousand golf carts here, he thought, and my security guys are doing a great job of keeping them corralled.

He reached into his cooler and pulled out two bottles of Prosecco and handed one to Conor, along with two wine glasses. "Carl, do you want a glass of Prosecco?"

"No thanks. I've got a lot of beer here. Anyone want a beer?"

Conor and Megan grinned. "You always think of everything, Dash," Megan said as she turned to Conor.

"You could take a few pointers from Dash, sweet husband o' mine."

Dash watched as Megan playfully kissed Conor's cheek. He thought with a twinge of envy, they are so lucky to have found each other.

When the fireworks began, he turned to look at Molly. Her face upturned and her eyes wide with delight she oohed and aahed at each explosion. She turned to him and smiled and he found himself smiling back at her.

"You should smile more, Chief Santorelli!" she said with a twinkle. "It makes you even more handsome."

CHAPTER 27

SATURDAY, JULY 11, 2014

"Dash, will you clear the table. I'll load the dishwasher and then we can sit out on the deck for a while."

Dash brought the plates, glasses and flatware and placed them on the counter. Molly rinsed them and put them in the dishwasher.

"No. Not my wine glass. I think I'll have another. Would you like one too?" asked Molly.

"Sure. I'll refill both of our glasses." said Dash as he retrieved Molly's glass from the dishwasher.

Molly and Dash took their wine glasses out to the deck. Stella followed them. They sat in the bench swing and swung slowly back and forth. Stella walked around in a tight circle several times until she lay down with a sigh.

They swung slowly back and forth.

"Look at the clouds." said Molly. The setting sun painted the few high clouds shades of pink, red, and magenta. The colors seemed to change by the minute.

"How do you like living in The Landings?" asked Dash.

"Well, it's not Brooklyn." Molly replied.

"Where did you live in Brooklyn? I lived in the City. I wonder if we were there at the same time."

"I lived in Park Slope my whole life until I started practicing medicine."

Molly went on, "I was a jock all through school. When I went to Brooklyn College, and took up jogging, joined a running group and ran marathons. I trained like a demon. Running empties the mind"

"What about your parents?"

"They were born in Germany and came to this country after the war. They're both dead now. My mom died when I was twelve. She had breast cancer."

"And your father?"

Molly remained silent for a while. "He's dead. I don't want to talk about him."

More silence.

"He was evil."

"What do you mean? Did he hurt you?"

"No. He was good to me. I didn't find out what he had done until after he died."

"He's buried in Cypress Hills Cemetery out on the Island -- quite near Eric Weiss, known as Houdini. I found boxes of photos at the back of his closet, on a high shelf. I wondered why he would have kept all those photos so secret.

I sat down with a glass of white wine and emptied the boxes on the kitchen table. I laughed and cried at photos of our life in Brooklyn. My mom was so young"

"Then I picked up the old sepia-toned photos from the time my parents were in Germany. I was born here, but my parents were German Jews"

"So there I was in my father's dingy little kitchen, photos all over his table, sipping my Chardonnay. Some photos were stuck together. I peeled them apart carefully.

139

The first one I looked at was taken in 1943. It showed a wintery, desolate background with rolls of barbed wire in the distance. Two men stood very straight, and proper, wearing black SS uniforms. My father was saluting a senior officer. I turned over the photo and read in very precise blue ink, 1943, Brigadefuhrer Hausser and Reichsfuhrer Heinrich Himmler."

"I snatched the rest of the bottle of Chardonnay off the table and drank the last two thirds of the bottle."

"I recognized my father in that photo even as a young man. He never spoke much about the War, saying only the camps were not for polite conversation. He had camp numbers tattooed on his forearm. I knew he had worked for US Army intelligence when he came to America. I always thought of him as a good man, a man outracing the Holocaust Satan. Now it appeared he *was* the Holocaust Satan - he and Himmler who'd invented the ovens which had been made by Mercedes. I know Jews who refuse to buy Mercedes to this day.

"That must have been a terrible shock to you."

He'd been a wonderful, loving father who'd bounced me on his knees and played ball with me in Prospect Park. It turned out he killed hundreds of thousands of Jews. *Oy vey.* I swept the photos into a paper bag and I then threw it into the smoldering living room fireplace. I watched the fire rage. Good Riddance."

"Dash, I've never spoken about this to anyone before. Not even Bob."

Dash put his arm around her and they were quiet as the swing moved back and forth.

The sun had set. It was so dark they couldn't see the marsh grass at the end of the yard, just steps away. The only sounds were the squeak of the swing and the deep hooting of a Great Horned owl from somewhere in the distant trees.

"Now, Mr. Donato Santorelli, famous detective . . ." said Molly in a lighter tone. "Tell me about yourself."

Dash looked at his watch and said, "It's getting pretty late. Maybe I should be heading home."

Molly turned to him and said, "Stay here tonight."

Stella lifted her head and looked at Molly quizzically.

CHAPTER 28

FRIDAY, AUGUST 22, 2014

Molly worked part-time as an Emergency Room doctor at Memorial University Medical Center. Her schedule had been in flux when she first had moved to Savannah and began to work there. Now, after twelve years, her schedule had settled into a more normal one. She worked Mondays, Tuesdays, and Wednesday from 8 AM to 4 PM unless the ER was slammed with an overflowing patient load. Then, it was all hands on deck.

She loved her schedule because it allowed her time to volunteer at the local library on the island, take Stella to the dog park, participate in Landlovers' activities, and to read. She was a voracious reader.

During the six months after Bob's death, she had worked her way through Proust's "Remembrance of Things Past". It was after she finished it she realized that she felt bad about Bob's death and still wondered how he had died. She really didn't miss him. She was in Savannah now, working just enough, and happy as a clam.

And then there was Dash.

She pulled out her cell phone and dialed Megan. "Are you free to join me on Friday for a ladies' day out? Lunch is my treat."

"I'd love to join you."

"I'll pick you up at 11:30 and the venue will be a surprise."

Molly and Meg made small talk on the drive from Isle of Hope to downtown Savannah. Molly pulled up to The Olde Pink House and Meg laughed.

"How did you know this is my favorite restaurant? Conor and I come here on special occasions, but I've never had lunch here."

After they were seated, Molly told her Dash had mentioned they treated him to dinner at the Olde Pink House the first time he had come to Savannah.

"Let's decide which of these yummy sounding dishes we're going to gorge on because I'd like to ask your advice about something." After they placed their orders, Molly told Meg she hoped she wouldn't think badly of her, but she wanted to talk about Dash.

"I don't know if you know, but Dash and I have been . . . dating. I guess you would call it that."

Megan laughed, "Oh, we do, we do. We're tickled pink. For Dash . . . and for you. You seem to get along so well. And, we've noticed that he smiles more. He tends to take life so seriously and he always throws himself into his work. There's more to life than work you know!"

Molly felt herself blush and she smiled. "We do get along well. We enjoy pretty much the same things. What we don't have in common, we're both interested in learning about."

"Here's the problem. He has asked me all about myself and I have told him my entire life story. At times I feel as if I am being interrogated. But when I ask him about his past, he seems to shut down. He makes me feel as if I'm intruding. I would never ask him about his past if he hadn't seemed interested in mine. He closes me out. Why won't he talk to me?"

"Oh, Molly. Conor and I have known Dash a very long time and that's just Dash being Dash. He's what I think of as the strong, silent type of guy, unlike Conor. Conor shares everything whether anyone wants to hear it or not."

Even though they are quite different, they think alike. Over the years, Conor and I have learned a bit about why Dash is the way he is, but it is for Dash to tell you, not me."

"What is the key to getting him to share his past with me? We have so much fun when we are together, but somehow I feel he is still a stranger."

"The answer, Molly, my dear, is patience. Patience, patience, patience."

CHAPTER 29

MONDAY, AUGUST 25, 2014

Dash answered his phone and Conor said, "You busy tonight?" Dash told him he had some reports to go over. "Forget 'em, my man. I closed a cold case today and Megan's got a hen party at the next door neighbor's. I'm on my own for dinner. Meet me at Johnny Harris's on Victory at 6 and we'll have some fine ribs and a few beers. See ya!" The call was ended.

Why not? Thought Dash.

He found Conor at the bar. Conor paid his tab and they were shown to one of the booths.

"This place is an institution, you know." They ordered and Conor asked, "So how's Molly?"

"Fine."

"That's all? Just fine? Come on, man. You've been seeing her for, what, a couple of months now. Right? That's longer than I've ever known you to date anyone. In fact, I only remember you going out with, two or three women over the last twenty-some years. You only went out a few times with each of them. Molly must be more than fine. Megan told me that she notices that you're smiling more. You've never been much of a smiler as long as I've known you!" Conor stared at Dash, waiting.

After a prolonged pause, Dash said, "She's nice. I like her. She's told me all about herself. Well, I guess I asked. She was married once, but only for three years. No children. But, when she asks about my past, I can't think of what to say."

Their dinners arrived and Dash took the opportunity to stop talking and immediately start eating.

"Whoa, there, boy. Those ribs aren't goin' anywhere. Why don't you know what to say to her?"

Dash continued to eat and just shook his head.

"Lookit! If you want to continue to see her, you'd best learn to share. Ya do know what that means, don't ya? Megan taught me that it's important to women." He chortled, "Sometimes she tells me that I share too much!"

MONDAY, SEPTEMBER 1, 2014

Dash put cans of beer in a tub of ice while Molly opened wine and set out glasses. They had decided to repay some of the many dinners they had had at the Donovans' house with a little party and had included Carl, next door, and his date, Stella.

"Oh, Dash, I'm going to have a terrible time tonight. How can I meet Carl's date and not think of my dog?" Molly giggled and smiled at him.

"Just don't say her name. Pretend her name is Fiona or something."

They both laughed and began to set out platters of antipasti. The doorbell rang and Conor and Megan entered. Carl walked into the kitchen from the patio with Stella. Dash looked at Molly and mouthed "Fiona" with a small grin.

The party was a success and by 9 PM, everyone had gone home. Dash and Molly started rinsing dishes and putting the few leftovers in the refrigerator when Molly yelped "Stella!"

"Shhhh. She might still be next door with Carl"

Molly said, "No, not that Stella. My Stella. I've got to run home before we finish cleaning up and let her out. Just sit down and turn on some music and I'll be right back and help you finish."

Dash took the dish towel off his shoulder and tossed it on the back of a chair. "I'll go with you. I don't like your going into a dark house by yourself."

Molly pulled into the drive and walked to the side porch. When she opened the door, they were faced with a fifty-six pound black and white parti poodle who was leaping like a kangaroo, tail waving like a cheerleader's pom pom and looking nothing like Carl's date. Molly turned on a few lights, went to the porch and unlocked the door. Stella leaped down the stairs to the back yard.

Dash followed Molly out on to the deck that ran the length of the house. They both looked out to the marsh at the end of the yard. The tide was high and a full moon shone on the water.

They both sighed and turned to each other. Stella tore back up to the porch and nudged between them, sat at attention and stared from one to the other.

Stella's heavy paw landed on Molly's foot. Molly stepped back to extract her foot and tripped on Stella's chew toy, losing her balance. Dash grabbed her shoulders and righted her. Their eyes met. Each of them began to speak and then stopped.

Dash drew Molly to him and leaned down to give her an all too brief touch of his lips on hers. "I'm sorry. I didn't mean to do that."

"I promised to go back to your house and help you finish cleaning up. Shall we go?"

"Let's just sit here and watch the moon for a while. Would that be okay with you? What time does Stella go to bed?"

Molly smiled and said "Right about now."

CHAPTER 30

TUESDAY, SEPTEMBER 2, 2014

What a crazy night, Molly thought. She had actually almost necked with him. Well, not really, but he had kissed her again and put his arm around her ever so gently. She didn't want him to leave. I'm acting like a teenager, she scolded herself as she grinned into the mirror. As she brushed her teeth, she looked at her hair. Silvery gray, cut in a short bob. She looked at her eyes. Grayish-green depending upon what she was wearing. Definitely green when she was wearing scrubs at work.

What could he possibly see in me? He is so handsome. That aquiline nose and those sad, dark brown eyes. He reminds me of Robert De Niro.

Oh, well, last night was probably just a one-off she thought as she grabbed her keys and headed to work. She backed out of the garage. She wondered if there could possibly be a two-off? She hoped so.

Her day had been fairly normal: high fevers of idiopathic origin, stomach pains needing to be diagnosed, broken bones, drug overdoses, and the usual number of gunshot wounds. Better hurry home and let Stella out.

Her iPhone rang as she unlocked the door. She looked to see who it was. The screen read Santorelli, D. She smiled and answered, "Hi!"

"Hi, to you, too. How was your day?"

"Normal, usual, and just fine. How was your day?"

"Great. Are you hungry?" Dash hoped.

"Of course, I am. I just got home from work. Stella! Stella! Come! Sorry she's going after a deer that just ran across my yard and into the neighbor's yard. I'd better get her! I'll call you back." Shooing Stella through the kitchen door, the phone rang. She grabbed it and said "Hello".

"Did you get her? Do you need me to come?"

"I've got her, but you are more than welcome to come. Let's go to Driftaway and celebrate our reconnecting there."

"How much time do you need?"

"Thirty minutes?"

"I'll be there in thirty." He said as he left his condo.

It was a Tuesday and Driftaway wasn't crowded. They decided to sit on the front porch. The other tables were empty. The waitress came and lighted the candle and asked what they wanted to drink. Molly ordered a glass of pinot gris and Dash ordered a Tito's martini with onions.

When their drinks arrived, Dash lifted his glass in a toast. "To our new friendship."

Molly repeated the toast and smiled at Dash.

After a silence, Dash said, "A penny for your thoughts."

"I've told you pretty much all about me. You're a man of mystery to me though. All I know is that you were a detective in D.C. There must be more to you than being a cop."

"Molly, I'm not very interesting guy."

"Tell me about your family."

"There was only me and my parents. They were both born in Venice. They worked at Harry's Bar, along the Grand Canal, near St. Mark's Square. The Bellini was born there and Carpaccio, too. Do you like Carpaccio? I wonder if we can find any in Savannah."

"My Mom baked the bread and my Dad waited tables. So many famous people came there. Toscanini, Chaplin, Hitchcock, Capote, Onassis, Orson Welles. My Dad would tell my Mom and me about them all."

"In 1948, a friend of my Dad's told him of a great Italian restaurant in New York City and that they were looking for authentic Italian waiters. He urged him to come to the US."

"My Mom found a job in a small bakery near their apartment in New York. My Dad was hired at his friend's restaurant, Patsy's Italian Restaurant on 56th Street near the theatre district. He began as a bus boy, but was grateful to have a job. Dad started bringing in Mom's homemade breads for the workers. Next thing my Mom was working at Patsy's, too, in charge of baking all their breads and rolls."

"As time passed, Gino, my dad, was promoted to wait staff. Management realized how skilled he was as a waiter when diners such as Tony Bennett, Frank Sinatra, and John F. Kennedy requested one of Gino's tables."

"When my parents arrived in America, they spoke and read enough English to get by. Reading Dashiell Hammett books helped them learn English. They were

151

the least expensive books at the nearby bookstore. They read aloud to each other. They both loved mysteries and they both loved to read. When I was born in 1950 my parents nicknamed me Little Dash in honor of their favorite author, Dashiell Hammett."

The waitress arrived with their dinners and silence reigned until Molly said, "Go on Dash."

"When I was four, we moved to Washington, D.C. Dad had such a good recommendation from the owner of Patsy's that he was hired as Maître d at Rive Gauche on the corner of Wisconsin and M Streets in Georgetown. It was the most elegant and expensive French restaurant in town at that time."

"I went to public schools in Georgetown. It was sort of easy for me. My Dad kept telling me that I should become a lawyer. He felt lawyers had the most power and money. I thought for a while I would become a lawyer."

"But you didn't." Why not?"

After a long pause, he said, "I've only talked about it twice before. Once, at the end of high school when I tried to explain to my parents why I was going to become a cop. The second time was after Conor and I had closed a long, ugly case. We went out to let off steam and relax. I let off too much steam and relaxed too much. Conor started to rib me about not having a girl, not dating, not being married, and stuff like that, and he wouldn't let up. I went postal. I tried to punch his lights out. Fortunately, he had a better and faster left hook than I did. The fight ended before it started. He saved me from myself. Conor wanted to know what that was all about. So I told him."

"The case we had just closed was almost identical to what happened when I was seventeen. What happened is why I'm a cop."

Molly waited, "Go on . . ."

After another long minute Dash said, "I know this is going to sound dumb or silly or whatever, but a long time ago I had a serious girlfriend. I think I fell in love with her in the fifth grade. She lived two blocks from our house. Her name was Ellie O'Donnell. She had Irish red hair and freckles. Her eyes were green. I asked her to the eighth grade dance and we began to date. I knew I would marry her someday. I couldn't imagine another girl as pretty or as bright as Ellie."

"One night when we were seventeen I took her to see *Fiddler on The Roof* at the theatre on K Street. After the movie we were walking to get ice cream. As we turned the corner, about half way up the block was an alley. When we reached the alley, two men dressed in dark clothes jumped out. One of them grabbed Ellie and the other grabbed me and slammed me down on the sidewalk. My head hit the concrete and I guess I was dazed or maybe knocked out for a second. When I was able to get up I saw them shove Ellie into a car idling by the curb. I got to the car as the last car door slammed shut and the car squealed off into the night.

Ellie's body was found early the next morning by a man and a woman walking their dog along the C & O Towpath, about a mile west of where I last saw her."

"Did they ever catch the guys?"

"No."

"The case Conor and I had closed the night I tried to punch him out was different in only one way. We got the perps." He made a fist. "That's why I became a cop."

"Oh, Dash. How awful that must have been for you. Your lives ahead of you and in one awful second . . ."

Molly's heart reached out to Dash as he stared at the table. She looked warmly at him and gently laid her hand over his fist. Gently, she turned his fist over and unclasped his fingers. "No more fists, dear Dash, no more fists."

After arriving home, Dash wandered around the condo like a panther on the prowl, upstairs, downstairs, out on the deck watching the little brown bats flitter to and fro, back and forth.

When Molly had said, "Hey, being head of Security in the Landings is a lovely job. So even-handed. No dramas. Smooth sailing, my dear, and at least you won't have to kill anyone." She'd smiled serenely, "Just making comments."

However that comment hit home and then some. Now, Dash plopped down on his comfy deckchair, the one he could get out of without clawing to get up. He ran a hand through his still-thick hair. His hand touched a short keyloided scar on the side of his head near his right ear and his mind catapulted to that far-ago night when the injury occurred.

He'd never told anyone that story and he never would.

CHAPTER 31

He and Ellie, at that intoxicating age of seventeen, walked under the moon and stars, enjoying their time together in their usually safe neighborhood.

Two men had come out of an alley. Dash felt a fist hit the side of his head, followed by another jab to his jaw. His head swerved involuntarily sideways. He heard Ellie's scream before it ended suddenly. As the pavement came up to meet him, a brutish hand grabbed him by his shirt collar and he stared into a man's face. The man's left eye had a scar starting from hairline and severing through the eyelid almost down to his top lip. What Dash saw was a milky white opaqueness of an actual eyeball.

"Motherfucker, you white guys got hard heads. And look here man, we be sharing this sweet piece a ass . . . motherfucker." The assailant's voice had a distinct Puerto Rican accent. Dash was certain.

If he made it through this, he'd spend his life hunting down this guy.

The next morning, as he dressed for discharge from the hospital after observation, a D.C. detective entered his room. "I'm sorry. I have some bad news. Ms. O'Donnell's body has been found."

Dash was speechless.

"We're still investigating."

A lethal focus suffused Dash's every pore. He would find Ellie's killers and he would effectively cut off the guy's lifeline. Come hell or high water. He painted an indelible image of the guy in his mind, a nasty-mouthed Puerto Rican with a white eye.

That promise to himself had taken years to fulfill, nine to be exact. Dash had become a D.C. detective before he had the slightest wind of Ellie's rapist/murderer. One of his C.I.'s out on the streets told him about a drug deal going down with this guy who called everybody, Whitey. Even the Mexicans and Blacks hated this weirdo with the milky eye.

"Hey man, I got sumpin. I got sumpin for ya. Whatcha got for old Toledo, here? Whatcha got, man? Sumpin for sumpin?"

For a long ten seconds, Dash stared at the guy. "Better be good." Then Dash fished sixty dollars out of his wallet and clasped Toledo's filthy hand as he pressed the money in the palm. The cash disappeared into a tear in Toledo's Salvation-style jacket.

Even then, before he knew anything, Dash felt his hackles rise. A prescient feeling of hunter and prey.

"Come on, Toledo, spill." Dash stared at a guy so skinny and hyped on crystal meth, he looked anorexic. His street-smart hands trembled almost violently as he fidgeted in front of Dash. Ignoring the guy's obviously poor physical condition, "You got something good. I wanna know. We'll see if you can't get a free pass next time you fence that shit of yours . . ."

Toledo's breath came out in a vile stream of air. "Yeah, Yeah. Good. Good. You my man. You is da Man, but you is a good man." Toledo ran on, his words jammed together with glistening spittle flying through the

156

air. "A deal, man. There be a big deal goin' down over dat big empty warehouse by da river tomorrow night. A bad Peurto Rican dude wid a white eye. Dude eats babies. He one nasty motherfucker. Word on de street, man, don't mess wid him."

There it was. Dash's moment of crystal clarity.

The next night, Dash and Conor Donovan, staked out the drug deal down by the Potomac. It took uncomfortable hours hunched down in-between rusting ship containers on the docks. Dash and Conor watched two shadowy figures. One passed a duffel bag to the other. Dash and Conor moved.

"D.C. Police!" screamed Dash, "Drop your weapons!" He aimed his .38 caliber Colt detective special revolver. He stared at the one guy's white eye.

Unfortunately, Dash and Conor were off the mark, standing at a tricky angle from the arrest. Both dealers took off running along the river. They split paths, but by now Dash had a bead on his target, Whitey.

Luckily, Conor took off after the other guy. "Halt you piece of shit, or I'll fire." Conor screamed as Dash sprinted after his prey.

Dash's breathing paced, his legs fell into an automatic runner's rhythm. A quarter of a mile later, over trash cans, cardboard boxes and assorted debris spilling down the river bank, Dash tackled Whitey with a well-aimed leap, so well-aimed he landed flush on the guy's back, effectively halting the guy before he could slip off the path's edge into the river. If Whitey got into the river with its fast surging currents and he could swim, Dash

157

would never be able to get him. Dash straddled the guy with one knee jammed into his back and handcuffed him. He flipped the tall, skinny guy over and peered into his face. The scar over his eye shone bright red against the creamy opaqueness of the blind eye.

"Remember me, motherfucker?" Dash hissed between clenched teeth.

After long seconds of confusion, Dash saw recognition register on the guy's face. "No. No, man. Wasn't me killed the bitch. You got da wrong guy."

Dash's breathing slowed. He lithely sprang into a stand. "Get up." Not a request.

Whitey struggled to get his legs under him, finally reaching a kneeling position. "Man, man these cuffs are killing me. Gimme a hand here. Hey man, we talk, yeah? Make good, yeah? Nuthin' a bit a talk won't fix." The Puerto Rican accent now sounded more American. One cheek and his mouth were abraded and embedded with dirt, gravel and blood. "Hey man, I getcha another bitch. No problema. We work like partners, man. You and me. We be sweet. We talk mano a mano, man."

Dash glared one time at the guy before he gave him a sudden shove off the steep slippery bank into the inkiness of the swiftly-moving river. "Have a nice trip, asshole."

Whitey's scream burbled with water. Soon, any sound had been effectively silenced by the forces of the currents. Black, swirling water pulled him down, down. Surviving with hands cuffed behind his back was a nonstarter.

"This is for you, Ellie my love."

Dash's official version went thus. He apprehended the drug dealer asshole, cuffed him and the guy slid out of Dash's grip and took off alongside the river. One misplaced step and the guy went over into the drink. Another scumbag at the mercy of Mother Nature.

Only Dash knew the real version.

*   *   *

Dash shook his head. Darkness closed around the pines with a soft, velvety cast. This total blackness always seemed to be hiding something from Dash. Hell. Must be just his cop's suspicious mind and besides, he needed to pee badly. The bats could fritter and flitter all they liked, Dash was going back inside his condo for the night. Tomorrow was a whole 'nother day.

The next day, sitting in his compact office on the second floor of the Main Gate building, Dash listened intently to his hand-held Motorola radio sitting on his desk. He had the ten codes down. These were used by all his Landings Security team.

Then static. "We've got a 10-31 in Oakridge. You want me to handle it, Chief?"

"OK, Jack. Go on over there." Dash spoke with his mouth close to his Motorola before setting it down again on his desk.

Motorola spoke to him a few minutes later. "Chief. 10-7." which meant the Security officer was on the scene. Followed a few minutes later by "Hey Chief, 10-8."

The scene had been cleared, the unsecured door shut with no drama.

Dash always breathed relief on these encounters: assisting fallen residents, corralling loose dogs, and checking out suspicious and unusual activities. Definitely not like being a detective on the D.C.P.D.

Since his people weren't armed, any domestic dispute or a similar problem required a call for assistance from the SCMPD. Domestic disputes could turn from a simple argument to murder in the time it took a heart to beat.

With his new security computer installations working well, Dash loved this job. Especially now he'd met Molly.

CHAPTER 32

CAIRNS, AUSTRALIA

MONDAY, JUNE 15, 2015

For the last few years every time Jock contacted Chu for an update Chu had a different excuse. This time it was the financial crisis in the United States that had dried up his financing. Before that it had been a strike at the ship building company in Korea where his ships were being retrofitted.

He remembered their last meeting. "Need more dollars, Mista Jock. At least five million . . ." Chu wore a confident smile. "Only five million more. You give ASAP." Chu said the letters slowly and with a big grin. He'd mastered colloquial English.

"Well, you know, I'll have to think about that Chu. I've already given you ten million and you want five more? I've only got one ship and the income from it is far less than what you predicted."

Am I being conned? How can Tommy Petroff be conned? I'm the best there is. But what the fuck is he doing with my money if he isn't buying ships?

"Chu need more money. We make much money together."

Jock paused, quickly rethought his position. "I don't have any more money to invest in your ships . . . My last investment made me a poor man."

Jock could feel Chu's rage.

This guy is dangerous. If I invest another five million I'll be down to my last million, . . . or maybe less. "No. Sorry Chu. No more money from me until I get what you promised me. No more money."

"I go now. You regret this Jock san." Chu abruptly left.

* * *

He called Chu and said, "No. No more money." Chu was furious. He argued on the phone saying Jock had made a commitment and couldn't back out now. Jock insisted that he had never made a commitment beyond the original ten million and accused Chu of squandering his original investment since he only had one ship to show for his investment.

The acrimonious phone conversation worried Jock. He was very concerned he had been stupid to invest ten million with Chu. I've blown two-thirds of my stash. Ever since I started Petroff Enterprises more than twenty years ago, I always had ample dough. Now I have to think about every cent, including the conversion rate to the Australian Dollar.

Grace had been born nine years ago. His beautiful daughter – another thing to think about.

Jock had his last six million wired from his offshore accounts to his account in Cairns. He thought it would be better to take some of that money . . . say three million and set up a trust for Grace.

He had lost confidence in Chu. He needed money in reserve while he waited for his investment to pay off. But now he wasn't sure that his investment with Chu would ever pay off. The only answer that kept coming up was to get back to America to find and retrieve his diamonds. They must be worth at least five million by now. Getting them back to Australia would be simple. He would just book passage on Captain Panama's ship. But first he decided to take care of Grace's future.

Christ, I'm not giving that bludgin' bastard one more red cent of my money. Who the hell does he think he is? He scoured his eyes with the heels of his hands. Jesus, now I'm thinking like an Aussie. Must have rubbed off after all these years.

CHAPTER 33

He did not notice the silent and seated Adams beside him. Adams could be in a room and you'd never know he was there. As now.

Jock sat restlessly and his eyes roved around the well-appointed waiting area in the offices of Burke, Burke and Wills. His eyes followed the geometric pattern of the thick carpet his crocodile boots rested on. The cushiony carpet ran sharp twists and turns in a muted but expensive grey and white. It was a perfect backdrop for his crocodile boots.

It seemed as if Chu had unwittingly pushed Jock into this position.

At first, after Chu had approached Jock for another five mill, Jock briefly thought about investing with the cagey bastard, but his old skills of accumulating and holding onto his money kicked in. Grace had already shot up to shoulder height. Next thing she'd be through high school and into University. His own blood.

"I'm going to be an ocean vet, dad. I'm going to save the whales   .   .   .   and dolphins and seals and walruses. All of them. I'm going to save them."

"Well honey. You're going to have to go to University to get a degree in oceanography, you know." He smiled at her and wondered how she'd sprung from his criminal genes.

His thoughts were rudely interrupted by a woman's voice. "Mr. MacInty, Mr. Burke will see you now. Please follow me." The woman had a voice like smooth caramel and she certainly didn't look bad either. Thin, with a small waist, hefty top, and a discreetly plunging neckline on her tailored green suit. She reminded him of Laura. He missed Laura, not just the diamonds. He had it all back in Connecticut, a mansion, a beautiful wife, a business that generated lots of cash. Now it was all gone.

Money begets money. Jock smirked at the thought as he and Adams followed the receptionist down a long wide corridor into the firm's plushly furnished conference room. Behind the dark mahogany table with light wood inlays, an entire wall was glass. His eyes slid down the stunning view of tropical greenery to a startling aqua ocean. Cirrus clouds brushed the azure sky. Pink, red and blue blossoms dotted and threaded their way through thickets of green. They were ten stories up. Apparently law pays too well.

"May I get you some tea?" purred the receptionist. She gestured to the silver tea service on the credenza.

"No, I'm good," responded Jock as his eyes gathered in all the artwork on the three walls. Matisse, Modigliani, what looked like a Seurat, a Manet and a Cezanne. Jock was pretty sure they were all bloody originals. He turned to Adams, seated politely on a cream-colored high-back chair. "Adams, you want tea?"

"Yes, sir. I think tea would marvelous." and he rose to go to the credenza.

The receptionist motioned for him to sit down with her beautifully manicured nails. She proceeded to pour Adams a cup of tea. "Milk and sugar?"

"Oh, a little milk would be a fine thing," answered Adams in his best English accent. "But no sugar. My waistline, you know . . . it's not what it used to be." He smiled warmly.

"We've done all your papers for the trust Mister MacInty. You're in the right place at Burke, Burke and Wills." Bill Burke leered at Jock more than smiled. "I have everything in order. All we need now are your two signatures. Jock MacInty and Ian Adams.

Not wanting to waste another billable minute, he picked up the Montblanc and scribbled his name and handed the pen to Adams.

He'd never really trusted lawyers, but . . . one had to do what one had to do. He'd already agreed to the lawyer's fees without blinking an eyelid. Four and a half thousand. What a rip-off. Jock figured they have to charge huge amounts to keep these richly-appointed offices with a view worth gazillions in real estate.

It's settled now. "Three million into a trust for my daughter, Grace. My friend, Adams, here will be the executor if anything happens to me. Not that anything will happen to me. I've covered all the tricky bases. My girlfriend, Alexa, knows nothing about this trust. She has absolutely nothing to do with the distribution of any funds."

If Alexa had anything to do with the trust, Grace would be left out in the cold. Adams will be Grace's Guardian. If anything ever happens to Adams, my old U.S. friend Molly Cohen, a doctor, will be Grace's guardian and executor of the estate.

Bill Burke notarized the signatures. He stood and handed a copy to Jock and a copy to Adams. "This is a solid estate plan Mr. MacInty."

As they left the office Jock said, "I didn't know your first name is Ian. Do you prefer Ian?"

"Adams is fine sir."

Adams, dressed as usual in his most formal attire, smiled warmly as his thoughts flew straight to Grace. The girl was like the daughter he'd never had and any protection she needed through life, Adams would be certain to give her.

"Right, Adams . . ." Jock interrupted Adams' thoughts. "I know that if anything happens to me, Grace will be in good hands."

"Absolutely, sir . . ." Adams never failed on the formality note.

It had all been under an hour. Jock wished he could charge four and a half thou for one hour's work. Probably had a blank Trust form already on file so the skulking lawyers could simply write in the numbers. Definitely not a losing line of work.

CHAPTER 34

On the way home from Burke, Burke and Wills, Adams drove and Jock read over the Trust papers again. Jock intermittently glanced at the passing scenery of trees in full blossom. Adams drove at a sedate speed which allowed Jock to inhale the heavily perfumed air of tropical Queensland. Mostly Frangipani trees. Grace's favorite.

Jock's convertible, the 2009 silver T Limited Edition from Bentley, made every drive so much better. Heads spun trying to get a look at the silver T gliding through the streets of Cairns. This was Jock's last big splurge for himself and Grace. She'd chosen the color because it reminded her of dolphin skins and the Eastern Grey kangaroo's fur.

The first thing he'd told Adams after they drove out of the Bentley dealership in Brisbane, "No one drives but me . . . and you." Grace only when she is old enough."

"Listen Adams," yelled Jock over the wind, "Alexa does not drive this baby. There are two sets of keys . . . yours and mine. OK?"

Adams demurred with British politeness, "Of course, sir."

"Yes. Yes. You can drive on our trip back home." Jock noticed the corner of Adams mouth turn up slightly, like a smile partially hidden back behind his face. "And next week, go out and get Alexa some cheap convertible to make her happy."

Jock felt the scented wind rushing through his thick head of hair. He always thought best when someone else was driving. His most innovative ideas came to him as he seemed to zone out and stare idly at passing scenery. He'd been mulling over the idea of a trust for Grace for months. Now, it had come to pass.

"Adams . . ." he said, pausing long enough to pass a bakery and have the aroma of freshly baked bread zoom up his nose.

"Sir . . ?"

Jock reveled in the delicious odor from the bakery. "Adams, you've worked for me for a very long time now. Grace loves you. I trust you."

"Yes, sir." Adams slowed the Bentley to a crawl as he took a side street in a residential neighborhood. "I am very happy where I am now. It is indeed a great pleasure to work for you and care for Grace." As if he knew Jock wanted to say more, Adams bit his lip in silence.

"There is something else you must know since you know most everything about us but not this." Jock ran his fingers through his now-knotty hair and yelped slightly as he encountered a wind-formed tangle. "Since you may turn out to be Grace's guardian at any old time . . . not that I'm thinking anything will happen to me . . . although, it is not out of the realm of possibilities. Pull over near that little park for a minute."

Adams expertly maneuvered the Bentley over near a bank of blooming flora and wild blue gumtrees. He cut the engine. Magpies warbled their glorious song to fill the air with a harmony beloved by Antipodians.

"I know I can trust you on this, Adams." Jock felt as if he was in a confessional and he wasn't even goddamn

Catholic. While I've been in Australia, I have gone by the name of Jock MacInty because it was imperative. In my other life, I wasn't known for my scrupulous honesty and there were many people out for my blood. So I disappeared . . . to keep the wolves at bay. Now . . ." Jock took a big inhalation and felt his heart trip over itself. "Should you ever have a need to find that doctor, Molly Cohen, you can only convince her of your situation by knowing my real name. She will know the name. I remember Molly was a good woman who seemed to have integrity and I envied her for that."

Adams had his right arm lounging, albeit professionally, over the side of the convertible. His other hand still gripped the steering wheel and he hoped he didn't look like he was holding his breath. "Anything you tell me, sir will be held in the strictest confidence."

"I know, I know Adams. I know I made the best choice of my life hiring you on. You and Grace have both made me look at my life . . . and the errors of my ways with brand new eyes. Hell, I never knew a Cassowary could kill you. I thought they were just some other exotic Aussie bird like an Emu."

"But joking aside, I want you to know what my old name was." Jock sucked in more air then said slowly, enunciating each syllable. "Tommy Petroff."

"Yes, sir. Tommy Petroff. I won't write it down. It's indelibly in my mind now. Your secret will be safe with me and Doctor Molly should the occasion arise."

"Right, Adams. Now get us home so we can have some grub - maybe prawns on the barbie as the Aussies say." Jock felt the weight of the secret leap free from his shoulders. He smiled.

He felt he was making personal headway since Australia had given him Grace and Adams. Now all he had to do was retrieve that whacking, great stash of diamonds . . . come hell or high water. Jock didn't care if they were blood diamonds or not - they'd still bring in a fair rate of exchange.

Adams pulled the car back onto the road and headed home. He was feeling his normal chipper self and hoped he would continue in good health for many more years to come.

CHAPTER 35

Jock hadn't given much thought to Laura since coming to Australia. But now he needed Laura. Rather he needed what Laura had, the statue with the diamonds. He needed a plan and he needed to know where that goddamn statue was. He went to his room and opened his Mac. He started to search for Laura. He couldn't find anything when he searched for Laura Petroff. He searched for Laura Higginbottom, but again nothing. He got on the Greenwich, Connecticut, government site and did a search for Treetops.

According to the Greenwich Times, Treetops had been sold in 1995 to the Stamford and Greenwich Land Conservation Trust and was now part of the Mianus River State Park owned by the Connecticut Department of Environmental Protection.

"Well, the bitch didn't waste much time getting rid of my house after I died," he mumbled.

He kept reading, but there was nothing about the former owners. Nothing about Laura. She was obviously gone. But where? How was he going to find her and the statue? He supposed he could hire a detective . . . but that left an obvious trail. So, no. No detective.

"Alexa bring me the bottle of Knob Creek and ice, sweetie."

He thought about calling some of his old acquaintances from Connecticut, but ruled that out because he was supposed to be dead. No one knows I'm alive except Les Mazza. Alexa brought his drink, set it on

172

his desk and getting no reaction from Jock, left the room. After his second drink he decided to see if he could track down Les.

First he ran an internet search for Mazza. He got a number of hits all over the country, but the only one that looked promising was a Mazza located in Jacksonville, Florida. Jock remembered Les loved hot weather. The entry listed a phone number with a 212 area code, New York City. It was 6:30 PM in Cairns and 8:30 AM in New York and Jacksonville. He grabbed one of his burner phones and dialed the number. No one answered, but he thought he recognized Les Mazza's voice on the voice mail greeting.

"Les, Jock MacInty here. Call me back at 61740511995." He poured his third bourbon and continued searching the internet for anything about Laura. Then he remembered that idiot sculptor who used to live in the studio on the Treetops property. He tried to remember his name but he couldn't. He knew the last name started with a "B". Bandage, Bandwith, Baneto, Bourbon, what was it? Then it came to him. Banderas. Yes, Banderas. He searched for Banderas and sculptor. There were over 500 hits. By now Jock had too much Knob Creek in him to continue the search. He fell into bed fully clothed and didn't wake for ten hours.

The next morning he woke feeling horribly hungover. The sun was too bright. His mouth was too dry. He felt nauseous. But he had work to do even though he felt crappy. Laura had to be found. He checked his cell phone for messages but there weren't any.

173

He went down to the kitchen and had Adams make him breakfast which he barely ate. After breakfast he took a cup of black coffee back to his room and continued his internet search.

According to the New York Times web site, Javier Banderas had retired to Savannah, Georgia. He checked the Savannah newspaper web site and was surprised to learn that Javier Banderas had married Laura Higginbottom in a small ceremony at some place called Bethesda in Savannah back in 2013. That's it. His Laura. He found her. But he couldn't find an address for Banderas in Savannah.

He went back to the article about the wedding. All he found was a statement that the married couple planned to live in the bride's home on Skidaway Island. He searched Skidaway Island and found that it was mostly occupied by homes in a gated development called The Landings. Jock couldn't get a list of residents because The Landings web site was password protected. Just then his cell phone rang.

"Yes" said Jock.

"Hey boss. How's tricks?"

"Les?"

"Yup. Should I call you Jock?"

"Yeah, still Jock. Listen man, I need your help. I'm trying to track down Laura."

I was right, Les thought. Jock must have left a stash of cash and Laura must know where it is. "Anything, boss, but my price has gone up."

Jock and Les eventually reached an agreement. As soon as Les found out where Laura was living he would text Jock and say: "I found the package." Jock would call Les back and get the details.

However, Les had his own idea. He would find Laura all right. That wouldn't be hard. But when he found her he would grab the cash.

Jock made up his mind he had to get back to the States as soon as possible so when Les called him he could grab the statue and get back to Australia. As soon as he got off the phone with Les, he called his travel agent and booked a first class ticket on the next available flight on Virgin Australia from Cairns to Brisbane, Brisbane to LA, LA to Atlanta and Atlanta to Savannah. Jock made preparations and told Alexa he would be going to the States the following day and would be back within a couple of weeks.

CHAPTER 36

SAVANNAH, GEORGIA

TUESDAY, JUNE 16, 2015

It didn't take Les long to find out Laura and Javier were living in The Landings. Savannah was a two hour drive up I-95 from Jacksonville. The snag was getting into the gated community. He didn't want Laura to know he was coming, so that ruled out going in as an invited guest. After some additional research he found out that service people were allowed to enter if they had a bar code sticker on their vehicles. Most of the utility companies had stickers.

He decided to pose as a Comcast Technician. They had bar codes on their trucks which allowed them to go through the gates without having to talk to guards. Comcast vans were ubiquitous. They went in and out of The Landings at will. He would need to steal a Comcast van in Savannah. One with a bar code. First he had to I.D. a Landings bar code. See what the thing looks like.

After Les moved to Jacksonville, he fell in with people in the drug trade. Jacksonville was a rest stop for drug runners moving product from Miami to New York. He wasn't into drugs, but found it helpful to know people in the trade.

On a stifling hot day, Les drove up to Savannah. He made a trip out to the Comcast main building west of town and parked in the visitor/customer lot. He could see the lot where the vans were parked. The fenced lot had an automatic gate with no guard. When the vehicles entered, the driver would insert a card in the reader and the gate opened. When the vans left the lot, the exit gate rose automatically.

Les came up with a plan to steal a van. He would return to the lot after midnight, hot wire the van and simply drive away. But he would have to scale a ten foot fence with rolled razor wire on top.

At sixty, Les was still in good shape. He ran on the beach in Jacksonville and was pretty sure he could scale the fence. The razor wire was the problem. It would be easier if he could get a local crew to steal the van.

He called one of his contacts in Jacksonville who referred him to someone in Savannah. He agreed to meet the guy at a bar on Waters Avenue. Les found the bar in a rundown area of the city. The smell of stale beer and smoke assaulted him. There were a couple of guys playing pool. Les opened his jacket so the butt of his .357 Magnum revolver could be seen. He didn't want anyone to think he was an easy mark. He asked the bartender, "Is Shanti here?"

The bartender nodded his head at a skinny guy with dreads and full sleeve tats on both arms at one of the pool tables. He approached Shanti and got right into it. "Jamal sent me."

"'S'up man?"

"Can you get me a Comcast van with a Landings sticker on it?"

"Hell, yeah. I can get'cha anything for a price."

Les agreed to pay him $750 up front and $750 when he turned the van over.

"OK, dude. Tomorrow night. Where do ya want it?"

"Park it behind the Day's Inn on Abercorn Street at 9 o'clock tomorrow morning. Tap the horn twice. I'll come out and give you the other $750." Les gave Shanti an envelope and handed him $250 from his wallet. Shanti opened the envelope and counted the 5 C-notes and added them to the $250. Shanti quickly pocketed the money and dropped the envelope on the sticky floor.

The next morning went as planned. Les drove the van out to Skidaway and easily made it through the unmanned gate using the bar code on the van. Using The Landings directory he found in the van, Les located Laura's address and parked in the driveway of the house next door. Les rang the doorbell and told the woman who answered he was looking for the Banderas house.

She told him they live next door, but they weren't home at the moment.

"That's OK. I don't need to go into the house. I'm working on outside cable connections. I have to make a few adjustments."

Les moved the van to Laura's driveway and walked to the back of the house. The rear of the house faced a lagoon. There was little chance he would be observed. He saw no evidence of a dog. Entering through the unlocked sliding doors, Les quietly made his way through the house.

He checked their home office, carefully going through the drawers in the desk, and quickly scanning their bank statements and other papers. If there was a safe, Les couldn't find it.

A laptop computer sat on the table behind the desk. Les moved it to the desk and started it up. He looked at her emails and document files, but none seemed helpful. He did check her calendar. He noticed that Laura was scheduled to work at the local library every Wednesday from 2:30 to 5 PM, and that she played golf on Thursdays. Javier worked at the Telfair museum every Monday, Wednesday and Friday from 10 to 5 PM.

Les checked his watch. He'd been in the house almost thirty minutes. I better get out of here before anyone comes home.

Right as he backed the van out of the driveway, he saw a silver Jaguar XKE coming up the street. The car turned into Laura's driveway.

After leaving Skidaway Island, he parked the van behind an old strip shopping center. He got out and looked around. No one looked at him. He took a razor blade and carefully peeled the bar code off the side window of the van. He pocketed the decal. At a nearby gas station Les called a cab. Before driving back to Jacksonville, he attached the bar code decal to the window of his truck.

* * *

Laura had finished her shift at the library and stopped at Publix. Fried Chicken, Javier's favorite. The chicken smelled hot and wonderful in the car. She pulled into her garage at 5:45 PM. She put the package on the island in the kitchen and went to the office to check her email. Didn't I close my laptop this morning? I'm sure I did. I thought I left it on the table. Christ, I hope I'm not losing it. Maybe Javier put it on the desk. Then she heard the garage door open. Javier must be home.

CHAPTER 37

IN THE AIR

WEDNESDAY, JUNE 17, 2015

First Class always produced the desired effect. More leg room, extra olives on a separate plate and the Martini pitcher served by eye candy flight attendants. Jock enjoyed the sleeper seats, extra thick blankets, down pillows, WiFi, and Kindles. He pushed back and brought up the leg rest. He mused about Grace, so far away.

His head sank into his down pillow as Grace rose into his consciousness. Thoughts of Grace transported Jock to a state of calm.

He could still hear the midwife years before saying, "Sir, your new baby girl is ready for a hold from her dad." The midwife handed over the tightly wrapped package with a cherub face and tons of black hair.

The moment he cradled Grace awkwardly in his arms, Jock knew nothing would ever be the same again. No one, not one single earthly inhabitant would ever lay a finger on Grace to cause her harm. His own flesh and blood had finally done to him what years of women and shifty business practices could never do. Becoming a father made him want to be a better man.

Grace became dad's girl right from the get go. Alexa seemed to know she'd been handed a second fiddle status, but the fact remained, Alexa was the mother of Jock's child, his cherished little Grace. So, as much as was humanly possible from a shopaholic Aussie woman, Alexa tried to take care of Grace. But mothering did not come naturally.

Adams cooked for the PTA fetes. Adams carpooled a thousand kids to hockey practice. Adams knew Grace's immunization history, her childhood diseases, her favorite snacks.

Jock and Adams shared fatherhood. Alexa shopped.

Jock took the child to kindergarten and picked her up four hours later. He'd take Grace to the beach where they'd walk out on the smooth, seaweed-strewn rocks at low tide observing all the rock pools filled with trapped sea anemones, crabs, starfish, mussels and assorted sea life. They'd walk along the white sand picking up Cowrie shells. Once they found a Nautilus shell. Jock had never built a sand castle in his life until Grace. Building one sand castle a day became a given. Now he and Grace could whip up a castle with turrets, moats, doors and windows. Jock tried to teach her how to take a photo of the sandcastles with his iPhone, but she already knew.

"Dad, can you smell the Frangipani flowers?" Grace chimed one day as Jock picked her up from Primary School. She looked like a perfect schoolchild in her light green tunic cinched at the waist, white short-sleeved shirt and a classic tie – mango and green striped. School colors. Black, shiny shoes and white socks completed her uniform. "They smell like our garden. All smelly and lovely." Grace made a big show of sniffing the air under a shady Frangipani tree heavily laden with creamy, white blossoms.

Jock made his own big effort to suck up the fragrant scent of the Frangipani blossoms. "Yes, they're like a good hug. Right? You want them around you all the time." He smiled down at his daughter.

"Dad, are we going down to the beach? I have a great idea for a sandcastle."

Jock always became stupefied when he gazed at his perfect daughter. "Whatever you want, honey."

"Well, I'm going to put starfish as windows on our castle and put crabs in the moat. That way when the tide comes in, everybody gets to swim home again."

How could Jock have ever produced this thoughtful, joyful child?

"And no one will interfere with your castle because there will be crabs in the moat," Jock offered with a smile.

She slung her heavy backpack into the back of Jock's Silver T convertible. He and Adams were the only two people allowed to drive it.

"One day you'll teach me how to drive dad, right?" she called over the wind as Jock barreled the Bentley towards the beach.

"You're not old enough, Grace," Jock smiled inwardly. "Of course, I'll teach you how to drive a stick shift, just as soon as you turn twelve."

"Dad, when you and mum went to Sydney, did you see Nemo?"

"Nemo? I don't know who you mean?"

"You remember, you took me to see the movie about the little orange clown fish who got lost. His father Merlin and Dory, she was the blue fish, searched for him all over and found him in Sydney harbor."

"Oh. Yes, honey. I remember the movie. We didn't see Nemo when we were in Sydney. I think he had already swum back out to the ocean with his father and Dory."

"I'm so glad."

"Dad?"

"Yes honey?"

"When I grow up I want to study all about the ocean and the things in it."

At thirty thousand feet, an air pocket of considerable magnitude almost rolled Jock out of his mostly supine position. His head snapped forward. That eye-candy stewardess began speaking in the plane intercom system. Jock sat up fully awake. The dream of Grace filled his heart.

He lifted the shade and saw that the plane was descending.

"Ladies and gentlemen, please fasten your seat belts, return your tray tables to their full upright position, and store your belongings under the seat in front of you in preparation for our landing in Los Angeles," droned the flight attendant.

CHAPTER 38

SAVANNAH, GEORGIA

WEDNESDAY, JUNE 17, 2015

Jock left Cairns early on Wednesday morning. By the time his flight arrived in Savannah, Georgia, it was late the same day although he had been traveling more than twenty-four hours. Pulling his carry-on bag, he went right to the Hertz counter. He collected the car he had reserved. With the aid of the GPS app on his phone he arrived at his hotel in less than an hour. He left the car with the valet and checked into the Hyatt Regency on Bay Street as Jock MacInty from Cairns, Australia.

"Hold my calls until I tell you." He told the receptionist. The bell hop took Jock to his room. He put the Do Not Disturb sign on the door and went straight to bed. He had slept on and off during the four flights, but needed some interrupted sleep. Jock had jetlag.

On Wednesday afternoon, Jock called the real estate company that handled most of the properties for sale at The Landings. He made an appointment to see some houses. The concierge gave him directions to Skidaway Island. He found the real estate office with the help of the officer at the gate. No problem.

While he was waiting for the sales woman, he took the opportunity to glance through the Landings residential phone directory lying on the table. He entered the address for Laura and Javier Banderas into his iPhone.

"Hello, Mr. MacInty. I'm Amy Thompson. Let's step into my office. Tell me what you're looking for."

"I'm living in Australia, but I'm looking for a second home in the states. I'm not married. No children." Jock flinched thinking of Grace.

"Perhaps you'd like a two or three bedroom house?" Amy offered.

"That sounds good. I'm interested in renting it out about six months of the year."

"No problem. If you purchase a house we can put it in the rental pool and take care of managing it while you're away.

Amy drove Jock around the community in her white Lexus. She toured through the village shopping area, the new Publix supermarket, the churches and the local library. Amy showed him the different areas of the Landings and the types and styles of homes in each.

"We have six golf courses, thirty-four tennis courts, two marinas, forty miles of walking trails, playgrounds, pools, and four club houses where meals are served. We also have a state of the art fitness center. There's no requirement to join the club but most do."

Jock just nodded and tried to look interested.

While they drove around, Jock saw mail trucks moving from mailbox to mailbox in front of the houses. He noticed all the mailboxes were the same color and size. Apparently the homeowners association had rules and regulations that reached all the way down to mail boxes.

186

The mail trucks reminded him of that summer job he had in college.

* * *

His job was to deliver mail in the same type of truck in Boston. God, what a summer. The sun, the heat, the car exhaust, the barking dogs. Federal rules required they take his fingerprints on employment. Cool. It was an easy job and paid well. He enjoyed riding around in a mail truck.

One day he finished his route early and he headed back to the substation. Thinking he was going to be praised for being so quick and efficient, Jock was surprised when the supervisor shouted at him.

"What on earth are you doing back here this early?"

"I finished the route." said Jock.

"Are you crazy? If a temp can finish a route that fast they're going to give the regular carrier more work when he comes back from vacation. Don't ever show up here before three o'clock. Got it?"

"Right. I got it."

Jock learned an important lesson. Hard work and efficiency were not always rewarded. After that, Jock would finish his route around noon and hang out in a bar watching the Red Sox on TV. He would drink beer until three or four o'clock. After which he'd would return to the substation and punch out. Paid by the hour, Jock wouldn't complain. If they're willing to pay me for sitting on my ass, fine.

* * *

Here he was now in Savannah with a real estate agent.

"Sorry? I didn't hear what you said."

Amy overtly glanced at her watch. With one had on the wheel and the other hand smoothing an eyebrow she said, "Oh, let's go look at some houses."

His real interest was to end the tour, get in his car and find Laura's house. He didn't know what he would do then. He couldn't go up to the door and ring the bell. His wife hadn't seen him for nearly eleven years. Besides, she thought he was dead. Still, he had to get his hands on the statue. He no longer needed Les to find Laura. Jock wondered if using Les had been a smart move. But he doesn't know about the statue.

Finally, Amy finished her house tour. Jock high-tailed it back to his hotel. He ordered room service and a bottle of Knob Creek and pondered ways could search Laura's house.

CHAPTER 39

While it was still dark, Jock drove back to Skidaway Island. He parked his car in the lot behind the Hallmark shop. Dressed in dark-colored running clothes, he began jogging toward the Deer Creek entrance. During his tour with Amy he noticed that gate was unattended. Jock jogged to Laura's street. He jogged several houses past Laura's and turned into a vacant lot. From there he made his way along a lagoon until he was directly behind Laura's house. No lights were on. He positioned himself behind a large Palmetto bush and watched the house.

After what seemed like hours, Jock heard the garage door open and close. After noting no activity in the house over the next hour, he cautiously approached the sliding glass doors.

What luck! They were unlocked. Jock stopped to listen for any sounds but heard nothing. He stepped into Laura's kitchen. He began going from room to room looking for the statue. He couldn't find it. The god damn thing was nowhere.

Unexpectedly, Laura stepped out of a room into the hall right in front of Jock. Jesus. God. Mother of mercy. His brain seized.

His phone rang. Reaching for it, he knocked it to the floor.

He was in bed in his hotel room in Savannah, Georgia. What a nightmare.

Jock picked up his phone. The text message read "I found the package."

Too late Les. Jock took out one of his burner phones and called Les.

"Boss. I found out where Laura lives."

"Good. Where?" asked Jock.

"She and that artist live at a place called The Landings on Skidaway Island near Savannah, Georgia. Her address is 154 Sun Dew Road. She drives a 2014 silver Jaguar and he drives a Saab convertible."

"Strong work Les. Anything else?"

"Yeah, the guy spends most Mondays, Wednesdays and Fridays at a museum in Savannah. Laura plays golf Thursdays and volunteers at a library on Skidaway Island every Wednesday from 2:30 until 5 PM when the library closes."

"Excellent!" said Jock.

"Why are you looking for her, Boss?"

Jock paused.

"Why are you looking for her?"

"Les? Les? Speak up. I can't hear you. Are you there?"

Les looked at the dead phone. "You son of a bitch!" He can't blow me off after I found Laura, his ex. He's up to something. She must have something he wants. Why else would he be looking for her?

Les decided to make another trip to Savannah. Maybe it's time for old Les to pay Laura a personal visit. The bitch will tell me what I want to know with some up close and personal persuasion. I don't believe I'll be sharing the information with Jock. But I've gotta wrap this up before Jock gets back here from Australia.

After hanging up with Les, Jock thought, now that I know their schedules I can get into her house and search for the statue. I'll wait until next Wednesday when both of them are out."

A plan formed in his head as he sat on the king size bed. Jock ordered room service. Twenty-five minutes later he heard a knock on his door. He opened it wide so the waiter could roll in a cart and set up his breakfast. It smelled delicious. He was starved. He had juice, eggs, bacon, toast and coffee. He still had jet lag and he really needed coffee.

As he ate, he noticed a red light on the wall near the window. It flashed. Peering at a sign under the light Jock read that it was intended to notify guests to ships passing by the hotel in the river. Jock flung open the drapes. He watched a massive ship with steel containers stacked eight high on its deck plying its way up the Savannah River. Jock had a third floor room and the containers on the ship were almost as high as his window. He felt as if he could reach out and touch it.

Could it be one of Chu's ships? Maybe Captain Panama is on board.

He tried to read the name of the ship, but missed it. He hoped Chu would deliver on his promise to purchase a fleet of these ships, but he had his doubts.

CHAPTER 40

Jock had heard good reports about Savannah, but had never visited the town. He had some time to kill before next Wednesday. Dressed in casual, comfortable clothes, he walked out of his hotel. The heat and humidity wrapped around him like a hot, wet blanket. No breeze at all. The Spanish moss limply dangled from the Live Oak trees in the squares. Sweat broke out all over his body. His shirt stuck to his chest as he walked around the Historic District and through some of the charming tree-filled squares. He stood in front of the building that General Sherman stayed in after marching his troops south from Atlanta during the Civil War. It was odd seeing history all around him, knowing he no longer lived in this country. A country that made him a rich man and also a fugitive from the law.

Near one o'clock he stepped into a touristy restaurant on the river for a beer, some shrimp and grits . . . a local specialty, but more importantly for the air conditioning. The cold beer tasted good. He didn't like the shrimp and grits. He missed Adam's famous carpetbagger steak.

After lunch he decided to take a bus tour. He chose The Old Savannah Tours. The driver gave a running commentary on the history of the city and pointed out places Jock would never have noticed on his own.

"If you look to the right" bellowed the driver over the speaker system, "you will see the house where Jim

Williams lived. Jim killed his lover Danny Hansford. This is the story that inspired the bestselling book *Midnight in the Garden of Good and Evil* by John Berendt. In 1997, Clint Eastwood directed the movie loosely based on the book with Kevin Spacey playing Jim Williams."

"Moving along, we are now passing Chippewa Square. See that bench? That's where Tom Hanks sat in the movie *Forrest Gump*. Other movies filmed in Savannah include *The General's Daughter* with John Travolta, *The Last Song* with Miley Cyrus, and for those who can remember 1962, the original *Cape Fear* with Robert Mitchum as Max Cady. That was quite a thriller."

The open sided bus slowly bounced over cobblestone streets and navigated the squares. The driver continued, "James Edward Oglethorpe first laid out the plan for Savannah in 1733. At that time there were four squares, Telfair, Ellis, Wright and Johnson. Currently there are twenty-one squares."

"Savannah is also noted for its haunted houses. One of the stories involves that building on the left, the birthplace of Juliette Gordon Low, the founder of the Girl Scouts. As legend has it, shortly after Juliette's mother Nelly died, the elderly butler told the family members who had gathered to mourn he had just seen Nellie's husband, William Washington Gordon II. William had been dead for five years. He said Mr. Gordon told him he had come back to get Miss Nelly. For those of you who want to learn more of the ghost stories, there are several tours, both walking and riding. Once upon a time you could take tours of the tunnels under St. Joe's hospital. It was super spooky."

Jock noticed the streets were filled with tourists walking around with maps and guide books in their hands or riding in other open sided tour buses. They were taking pictures of buildings, tour buses, horse drawn carriages, wrought iron railings, fountains, and themselves.

He got off the bus and toured several historic houses. On the next bus he continued his tour. He thought he wouldn't mind living here if it weren't for Laura. But he was here to do a job.

He ended his bus tour at the Telfair museum. The Jepson Center, a modern glass and stone-sided museum stood next to the Telfair. He and Laura regularly visited the museums in New York – The Guggenheim, the Metropolitan Museum of Art, MOMA, and the Museum of Natural history. He thought about going in the Jepson, but remembered Laura's new husband, the slimy Spanish bludger, Javier Banderas volunteered there. No way did he want to run into him. Despite the surgery, Jock didn't want to risk it.

Strolling down Broughton Street he noticed a long queue of people outside an ice cream store, Leopold's. If the line hadn't been so long he would have tried the ice cream to find out what all the fuss was about.

A little girl and her mother walked out of the store into the heat. The girl clutched a rapidly melting ice cream cone. She looked to be nine or ten, about the same age as his Grace. Oh, how he missed Grace.

CHAPTER 41

WEDNESDAY, JUNE 24, 2015

Jock thumbed in the number for the Landings Real Estate Company.

"Good morning, the Landings Company. How may I help you?"

"I'd like to speak to Amy Thompson."

"I'm sorry she is out of the office today. Can someone else help you."

"This is Jock MacInty. Amy showed me some houses last week and I wanted to look at some of them again. I can be out there by eleven. Do you have an agent available?"

"Yes, absolutely Mr. MacInty. I will leave a guest pass for you at the main gate. Come over to our office and I will have an agent take you around."

"I'll see you later." Jock hung up. His old personality creeping back.

The next call he made was to the Telfair Museum. He asked for Javier Banderas. He was told to hold.

"*Hola.* This is Javier Banderas."

Jock hung up.

He then called the Village Library and asked for Laura Banderas.

"She's not here now but she will be coming in today at 2:30."

Jock thanked her and hung up. Next, he called the hotel valet and asked that his rental car be delivered to the valet stand. Jock left the hotel at eleven and stopped at a shopping center not far from Skidaway Island. He felt a little peckish. After a Subway sandwich and a large Coke, he drove onto Skidaway Island and past the Village Library to make sure Laura was working. He saw a silver Jaguar parked across from the library. Jock pulled up at the main gate. "I have an appointment with the real estate company. They said they would leave a pass for me."

"If you would kindly show me your driver's license." said the guard.

Jock felt his pulse race as he pulled out his wallet and handed the guard his International Driver's License.

"Well", said the guard as he looked at the strange document, "I've never seen one quite like this. You're a long way from home. You actually live in Australia?"

"Yes, but I'm thinking of moving here."

"Oh, you should Mr. MacInty. This is a great place and the weather is nice. No snow. But I suppose it doesn't snow much in Australia either." The guard wrote Jock's information on his clip-board, walked around the back of the car and wrote down the license plate number on the form. He returned Jock's license, smiled and wished him "G'day mate." as he raised the gate.

Jock drove in, but didn't go to the real estate office. He headed straight for Laura's house. In front of Laura's house he noticed a lawn service truck and trailer. One guy drove a mower up a ramp into the trailer while the other guy finished blowing the driveway. Jock parked a couple houses down and waited until they drove off. Jock strode up to Laura's house as if he belonged there. He proceeded to the back of the house.

It must have rained last night. Shit, my shoes are getting soaked, he thought.

Jock tried the back door. Locked. Moving on to the sliding glass doors, he found them unlocked and entered. He looked around the family room. No statue. He went down the hall and searched the bedrooms. No statue. He ended up in their home office.

Nicely furnished with a couch, a walnut desk with a reading lamp and a credenza behind a large leather chair. Book cases lined two walls and framed paintings covered the wall behind the desk. It reminded him of the library in Treetops. He scanned the book shelves. No statue. He sat down at the desk and opened the drawers. He looked for any bank records or anything that would show him if she had found and sold the diamonds. He didn't see any deposits large enough. He moved the laptop from the credenza to the desk and went through the documents stored on the computer. Again he found nothing helpful.

Swiveling the chair so it faced the wall behind the credenza, he saw a picture of Laura and Javier with the notation 'Telfair Charity Ball 1997'. He saw several framed photos of Laura with other women posing at various golf tournaments. Runner-up. 'Nine Hole Tournament 2005'. Most improved foursome 2001. A certificate from the Landings Club congratulating Laura for a Hole-in-One in 2011. Another certificate from the Landings Association for Volunteer of the Year 2007.

Then he noticed a wooden plaque at the far right side of the wall. He couldn't read it from his chair so he got up and took it down and laid it on the desk. He turned on the desk lamp to read the inscription.

On behalf of THE VILLAGE LIBRARY, I thank you LAURA BANDERAS for your generous donation of 'Child with a Book' created by the renowned sculptor, Javier Banderas. We will proudly display this artistic treasure.
Sue Sturges, President.

Now I know where it is, thought Jock.

*   *   *

Laura came home after her shift at the library about 5:30 on Wednesday. She noticed the family room was unusually warm then saw the sliding door partly open. Looking down at the Persian rug which had cost her a mint, Laura immediately saw a clump of recently-cut grass near the sliding glass doors. Remembering she had found her computer open last week when she returned from work, she called security.

Two Landings security guards arrived shortly. Laura told them someone had been in her house. She showed them the trail of grass clippings in the family room leading to the hall. One of the guards, a tall bald man, introduced himself as Sonny Miller. He asked her if anything was missing.

"It doesn't seem like anything is missing."

Miller asked her if she had any guns in the house.

"Gracious, no."

She showed them into the office and told them how the computer should have been on the credenza, not the desk.

"Also, that plaque on the desk should be on the wall."

"There have been some home invasions recently. They usually take cash, jewelry, sometimes computers and guns. We think kids are behind the incidents."

Javier burst through the front door. "Laura, what is that security car doing in the driveway?"

Laura and the guards came out of the office and she told Javier what had happened. The guards edged toward the door.

Laura asked, "Aren't you going to take fingerprints or anything?"

"We don't do that, ma'am. We're just private security. If you want, we can notify the Savannah-Chatham police, but in a case like this where no one was hurt and nothing was taken, they probably won't do anything." Miller suggested they get new locks on the sliding door and perhaps consider installing an alarm system.

Javier said, "No need to report it. I'll arrange to have an alarm installed."

Miller gave him his card. "Please call me if you find anything missing."

Laura clutched his arm. "Javier, I'm scared. Last week I noticed the computer had been moved from the credenza to the desk and left open. Did you move it?"

"No, no. It wasn't me, *cara*. I never touch your computer. Donna worry. Tomorrow before I go to work I get an alarm company out here to install something."

CHAPTER 42

WEDNESDAY, JULY 29, 2015

Ever since Merilee moved in next door to the debonair artiste, she'd been certifiably happy.

"Yoo hoo," she'd trilled on the first morning she'd seen him retrieving the Wall Street Journal from the end of his lengthy circular driveway. He'd been almost obscured by a plethora of blooming Lantana stalks.

"*Hola,*" he'd murmured looking around. He'd been thinking he'd build a sculpture for a spot right at the end of the driveway, exactly where the paper carrier always flung the newspaper.

"Javier, isn't it?" Merilee popped around a trunk of a live oak, as if she'd spent the night there . . . waiting for his morning arrival . . . like an art groupie.

"I've seen you around since we live next door to each other. I saw your wife leave and I thought I might interest you in a yummy breakfast of crepes with a mug of straight, strong espresso." She stressed the words, "straight and strong." She smiled one of those smiles a shark gives you before it bites into your juicy thigh muscle.

"My wife, Laura, she is a very jealous woman." Javier noticed her eyes did not seem to move when her mouth smiled. How odd is that? However, since Laura is away this morning, already out the door and off to her nine-hole golf game, perhaps Javier would indulge himself.

"Maybe I could perhaps join you for a quick coffee. You have no cats, do you? I am highly allergic." He thought she looked the type to have cats.

"Not a chance. They're just too sneaky for me. My late husband had a Russian Blue . . . and that bastard took it with him."

They trudged up the twenty front steps to Merilee's mansion which overlooked a picturesque lagoon completely choked with waterlilies, reminiscent of Monet's Waterlilies.

As Javier walked into her house, he thought he saw something scurry under a sofa. No, he must be seeing things. Maybe she did have cats.

"Was that a cat?"

"No, I told you I don't have a cat. Come sit. Coffee's ready."

They sat down at her kitchen table.

As he set his cup down, not one, but two white-faced, tawny-furred bodies slinked up onto a vacant kitchen chair and stared at Javier.

Javier choked on a mouthful of coffee and coughed it out all over his favorite shirt. Merilee handed him a paper towel and he delicately dabbed his mouth and shirt. "What is zees? Invasion of zee exotic?" He coughed again.

The tiny creatures calmly stared curiously at Javier.

Unfazed, Merilee said, "Oh, these are my babies, Fredericka and Fournier. They're white-faced ferrets and very affectionate. No shedding. Very clean. Not at all like cats. My ex-husband wanted them, too. Can you imagine, he wanted the cat and my ferrets? I had to fight for custody. That man was a psychopath."

Merilee remembered how her husband's off-shore bank accounts had simply disappeared when it came time to divvy up. If she could nab Javier, her luck might change - art-wise at least. She didn't know a Keith Harring from a Robert Rauchenburg. Javier's wife seemed oblivious to having such a handsome, artsy husband, so maybe she had a chance.

They're not cats, but I still don't want to sit and drink coffee with them. He started to leave.

"I've seen pictures of your sculptures. They're beautiful. I don't suppose anyone like me could afford to buy one."

*   *   *

Merilee kept getting stuck at the library working with Javier's wife. What was her name again? . . . Lana, Lizette, Laura? Something ordinary.

"Oh, hi, Laureen," Merilee piped up on their practically simultaneous arrival to take over the library for the 2:30 to 5 PM shift. "I love working with you. It gives us a chance to chit chat. We're neighbors, but we never seem to have time to chit chat, Laureen."

"It's Laura. My name is Laura," replied Laura through clenched teeth. How could she abide two and a half hours with this woman? Especially since Javier wanted to give that stupid, little bronze statue to her.

Promptly, the day Javier mentioned giving the little bronze statue to Merilee, Laura rummaged around the house for the thing. She found it buried at the back of her linen closet. She dragged it out and dusted it off. Forty minutes later, Laura had given it to the Library President who'd just happened to be volunteering at the desk that morning.

"Laura, you are so very generous. We're so fortunate you and Javier moved to The Landings. And even luckier you decided to become a Library volunteer," the President had beamed, and clutching the statue to her bosom.

Done. Now, the statue sat displayed prominently above the most recently published popular fiction.

CHAPTER 43

THURSDAY, JULY 30, 2015

At precisely 10 AM the house phone had rung and without looking at the Caller ID, Laura swiftly picked up.

"Helloooo?????"

"Is this Laura Petroff?"

"Not Petroff anymore," she automatically responded, "who is this?" Somewhere in her atavistic brain the voice seemed familiar despite the fact it had a distinctive accent. She tried to conjure the name to the fore.

The caller hung up.

Laura looked at the phone. She felt her armpits turn damp despite "Perspiration Stop Natural Crystal" underarm. She gently put the phone down and stared at it.

This was absolutely ridiculous. Her mind must be playing tricks with her. Another good, strong drink is what she needed to stop her hands shaking. Probably a vendor or someone wanting a donation because everyone knew she wasn't hurting for greenbacks.

* * *

Jock sat in his rental car parked in front of The Village Library. He put his phone back in his pocket. Laura's at home, so now's a good time to see if the statue is really in the library. He stepped out of the car and ground his cigarette under his foot. Casually, he walked up to the entrance of the library. Upon entering, he saw a large desk. Over the desk was a cupola with light streaming in through windows set high on the walls. A woman sat at the desk facing the front door. She busily worked at her computer while an elderly man waited to check out a stack of books. Another woman had her back to Jock. She stared out the glass paneled rear doors at a lagoon with lily pads and Double-Crested cormorants.

The woman working on the computer called out in frustration, "Molly, I can't seem to find out why Mr. Thompson has a sixty cent fine on his account. Can you help me?"

Molly stood up from the rear facing desk and came over to help. She leaned over to look at the computer screen and said, "First, you need to pull up Mr. Thompson's account. Then click on fines at the bottom and that will tell you why he was charged sixty cents."

"Mr. Thompson the charge was incurred for a rental book. We charge thirty cents a day for those. You had it for two days and that is why the computer shows you owe sixty cents."

"Oh, very well. Here's a dollar. You can keep the change."

Mr. Thompson left, his arms loaded with books. Molly returned to the back desk to help another patron. Jock thought he recognized Molly, but he wasn't sure. After Mr. Thompson left, Jock stepped up to the desk.

The volunteer's name tag said Diane Hopkins. She asked, "May I help you?" She looked to be in her late sixties, thin, with gray-white hair and a pleasant grandmotherly smile on her face.

"I'm new in town. Do you mind if I just look around the library."

Diane said, "What a charming accent. Where are you from?"

"Australia."

"I can show you around if you like."

"No. No. I'm fine. I'll just browse."

"Be our guest. If you would like any help just let me know." replied Diane. He didn't seem very friendly.

Jock walked around the main room moving between the rows of book shelves and barely glanced at the books. He wandered toward the rear of the room where he spotted a statue of a child reading. It sat on top of a low shelf of books just below a window. Endorphins flooded his system immediately. He tried to control his excitement. He carefully picked up the statue and examined it closely. This was the statue that he had hidden the diamonds in all those years ago. He surreptitiously glanced around.

There are too many people in the room. Bloody hell. I can't check it out now. He replaced it on the shelf and walked to Diane's station.

"This is a very impressive little library. Maybe you could show me around." He didn't care about joining the library. All he was interested in was seeing the layout, whether they had any security, and where the doors were located.

"Oh, yes. I'd love to. Diane enthusiastically rose. She handed Jock a library bookmark. He stuffed it in his pocket. She began a rehearsed orientation she gave to new members.

"The library has a collection of over 25,000 books. All of the books in this main room are fiction organized by author's last name. She led him into the children's room droning on about the programs offered for children.

As they walked toward the new wing they passed Molly helping another patron. He glanced down at her name tag and read Molly Cohen. His suspicion was confirmed. Yup. I knew it. I was right. That is Bob Hathaway's widow, Molly.

Diane walked Jock down a long hall past framed paintings on one wall and windows on the other wall overlooking the lagoon. They passed a small seating area and entered the new wing.

"Non-fiction, biography, large-print books, and audio books are in this room. Over there are used books for sale."

Jock looked at the ceiling. No cameras. He spotted a door marked: office. "Diane what's in there?"

"That's where the volunteers process the new books and the used books. This entire library is run by volunteers. We have no paid employees. Some of our operating income is derived from the sale of donated books."

Jock opened the door and walked passed her into the office. There was no one in the room. Jock looked around. Again, no cameras. He noticed a white board showing the month of September hanging on the wall.

"I'm really not supposed to let you in here."

"What's with the calendar?" asked Jock. Molly's name was written in on each Thursday and Laura's name was each Wednesday.

"That's the calendar the volunteers use to sign up for their shifts."

"Where does that door lead?" asked Jock pointing to the exit door.

"That door opens onto the street. Volunteers use it to leave after locking all of the other doors at the end of the day. It locks automatically."

The exit door did not appear to have an alarm.

"What time do you close?" asked Jock.

"We are open from ten until five each day except Saturday when we close at 2:30. The first volunteers come in at 9:30." said Diane. "The hours and our phone number are on the bookmark I gave you."

Jock walked out of the office and back into the library.

Diane closed the door and they proceeded back toward the main room. Jock noticed Molly was not at her desk.

"Thank you, Diane. I don't want to take up any more of your time. I enjoyed the tour."

As Molly walked passed them to her desk Jock smiled and looked down at her name tag. "Molly Cohen.

I knew a Molly Cohen a long time ago. Are you from Washington State?" Jock looked directly at Molly.

Distracted, Molly glanced up at him and said, "I'm afraid not. I've never been there." She gave him a quick smile and went to her desk.

Walking out to his car Jock thought, I've killed two birds with one stone. I know where Molly Cohen is and I've found the statue.

"Diane, who was that man you were showing around?" asked Molly. "He seemed kind of familiar, but I can't place him."

"He didn't tell me his name. He's not a member. He said he was from Australia."

CHAPTER 44

TUESDAY, AUGUST 4, 2015

Laura scrubbed her face with DHC Deep Cleansing Oil, splashed on tepid water to remove it, and expertly rubbed in L'Occitaine Night Cream. The scent from the night cream drifted up her cute, pert nose compliments of Dr. Swan's scalpel many years ago. Tomorrow, she told herself, she'd go for an early morning massage at the Fitness Center. Afterwards, perhaps, she'd go downtown for a quick trip to the Jepson Museum then to the Hilton to meet with her new flavor of the month guy who was willing to do anything for her, wear white tighties instead of boxers, even clean her pool in a thong. All this for an introduction to the Javier Banderas, sculptor of bronze. It wasn't only the Savannah elite who loved him, even her pool boy wanted an introduction. He was in high demand here in the southern climes.

Speak of the devil. Javier wandered into her bathroom without knocking or even announcing his entrance. Did that man have no manners?

"Laurrra," he rolled his "r's" in that Spanish way he thought was adored by Laura. "My Sweet, tomorrow I must go to Charleston for the new Gallery Banderas opening. My pieces, you know, they are already selling every place down here in the South. Come to my studio. I can show you my latest piece. I'll make a few small donations to the Jepson Museum, too. They made me a

Board member. Now I am what you call, an American celebrity." he grinned wolfishly. Javier stood six feet two inches and was solidly built with an eternal tan lending a swarthy, artistic bent to his features. And he knew it.

"Follow an American celebrity to his studio, *cara*," he brushed her cheek with his lips.

She inwardly recoiled. This meant he wanted a little skin to skin arrangement or he'd throw a tantrum and complain his conjugal rights were being denied.

"Sorry, Javie. I have a doctor's appointment downtown tomorrow. I need my beauty sleep as they say. Perhaps next week I could come with you to mingle with that uppity Charleston set.

Javier hated being called "Javie" though he had never said as much. She felt him cringe every time she said the word and it brought an inner smile to her.

She had begun giving away as many of his "pieces" as she could without his noticing. The Village Library president had positively gushed when she presented them with that bronze statue of a child reading. She had needed to get rid of that particular piece for two reasons. The first, because her late husband, Tommy, (God rest his swindling soul.) He had left her a veritable fortune and really loved that statue. He had commandeered it from her to sit on his office desk and with no intention to return it to her.

The second reason, Javier scooped it back up when they moved to The Landings, saying, "It would look so delightful catching the morning sun in the front window of Merilee's house. She needs a sign that people still care about her since her husband passed on."

Merilee's husband truly had "passed on". He had left her for another shark-minded, fund-raising queen at The Landings. Now, Merilee thought the sun shone out of Javier's lower reaches and was shamelessly brushing against every inch of the man. She would come over to borrow a cup of sugar, or rice, or milk, or anti-freeze, or drain cleaner, or any goddamn thing she could think up.

She wanted to take Javier to her book club. Laura laughed at the thought of Javier at a book club filled with The Landings female literati.

Anyway, she gave the little bronze statue to the Village Library within a year of their move to The Landings. It was then she decided marrying Javier would be the only way to keep the flood of single women . . . and married . . . off his radar and out of her hair. It was also at that very time, she signed up to become a Library Volunteer which had turned out to be something she really, really liked doing. Quite a surprise to her.

She had an appointment for a soothing mani/pedi with those delightful professional apprentices of Stephan at the Heavenly Hair Salon on Broughton Street tomorrow. Perhaps she could squeeze in a wash and blow dry too. Stephan was a wiz at highlightening her shoulder length blonde hair.

Her thoughts returned to Javier. She had loved him during all those throbbing hot years in Greenwich, Connecticut. After all, he was one very talented sculptor. His popularity had risen exponentially since they'd come to Savannah. At a perfectly normal dinner party one night, no less than nine women had surrounded him and essentially offered him their services as models for his bronzes. It seemed every woman in The Landings had set her sights on him. That was why she'd had to marry the man.

However, marriage to the artist himself had still come with certain baggage. "Money talks." was Tommy's mantra. Since Laura had money, she made it abundantly clear to Javier she wanted her own suite in the house, her own bedroom, bathroom, drawing room, and balcony. She wanted a cleaning crew once a week and a catered dinner party once a month in order to show off her coveted Harry Winston diamond ring which her late, dear departed had bestowed upon her with a little encouragement on her part.

This arrangement left Javier his own suite which he'd immediately turned into a studio of the expensive type. He'd hired a decorator, Suzanne the Sexpot to "decor" his suite. Suzanne still frequently called, even though the renovation was long ago completed.

"*Cara*, come with me." whispered Javier in Laura's ear, his bourbon breath hot and snaking up her nose.

She looked up at him and settled more comfortably on the stool she'd put in front of the mirror. She saw he was heavily "in the bag" as Tommy used to say. Laura hated the way inebriation made him think even more highly of himself. His ego was fueled by alcohol and women.

"Come to think of it, perhaps I will see you in a minute. Go back to the studio and I'll bring you a nightcap." She winked at him.

Feeling victorious, he strode out of her bathroom.

Laura stood, snatched a tiny bottle out of her make-up collection and headed for the bar in the den. She poured a healthy shot of Woodford Reserve Kentucky Straight Bourbon, Javier's absolute favorite since he'd been in the U S of A. In a heartbeat, he'd expound on why Bourbon County, Kentucky, was the only place on earth where real bourbon is made. My God, the man was a Spaniard and here he was waxing poetic about an American liquor.

Laura added two 10 mg tablets of Valium, stirring with a Waterford crystal swivel stick until they were completely dissolved. Then she poured a drink for herself, sans Valium.

"Javie, my pet." Laura handed Javier his glass as he swarmed around one of his current bronzes.

He took the glass. "Salud," he muttered and touched her glass before he chugged back the entire glassful. "Why you must call me "Javie" my Laura? It is so . . . so . . . common, common like that," said he with a flourish, pointing to a mass-produced wrought iron plant holder in Merilee's garden with fairy lights. It glowed like nuclear silo. "Like this *de mal gusto*."

"I meant it only as a loving name, Javier, my sweet husband." she smiled beguilingly.

It took at least ten minutes before he stopped groping Laura and lay back on his king-sized bed to "rest his head for a little bit . . ."

Laura pecked Javier's cheek and headed back to the den. Mission accomplished. Tomorrow she could be alone, well not alone, but not with him. When she saw Stephan at the salon, she might have him change her hair back to a nice, coppery auburn. She was tired of being a highlighted blonde.

She walked into the den where she'd left her iPad on the coffee table. Oh my lord, tomorrow at 2:30 is my day to volunteer at the Library. She had almost forgotten all about that. Heaven knows, she didn't want to give those people anything to gossip about, especially since she was working with that non-stop talker, Merilee.

The following morning Laura noticed Javier had gone. He left her a pot of steaming hot coffee. She had waited to venture into the kitchen until after she heard the garage door open and close. He really did seem to love her. Bless his heart. That was an entirely appropriate thing since none of those other fawning women came close to Laura's standards. She'd make it up to Javier tonight when he came home.

CHAPTER 45

WEDNESDAY, AUGUST 5, 2015

Abruptly, Jock woke from a deep sleep in his bed at the hotel in Savannah. *Where am I? His phone continued to ring.* His arm reached out and knocked the clock radio off of the night stand on to the carpeted floor. Jock sat up in a daze and reached for his iPhone. *It was a 904 area code.*

"Yeah?" he breathed into the phone.

"Hey, Boss it's me, Les. I've got more info on Laura. What do you want to do?"

"Forget Laura."

"But, Boss, I can still help. I know where she lives. I know her daily schedule. She's married. Did you know that? She married that sculpture guy that used to live on your property up in Greenwich."

"Forget it, Les. I'm fine here in Australia. I have a new life. Never mind Laura. I'll send you the money for the work you've done, but forget Laura. Let her live her new life." Jock touched the red circle at the bottom of the iPhone screen and ended the call.

Les looked at his phone. Then he looked at the tracker app on his phone. *He's in Savannah, not Australia. Those coordinates are centered on the Hyatt Regency Hotel. He's definitely come back for Laura. She must have something he desperately wants*

"Thanks. Just put it over there." Jock handed the room service guy five dollars and ushered him out. Jock sat down to eat his breakfast. As he chewed, he thought, I told Les never to call me on my iPhone. What's he up to? I gotta get those diamonds fast and get out of here. It's gotta be tonight. There's no telling where Les is or what he is planning. I know Laura is supposed to work today. I'll get there before the library closes. When she leaves at 5, I'll grab the statue, palm the diamonds, and then Bye, Bye Miss American Pie.

When Jock finished eating he took a shower, dressed and packed his suitcases. He ordered his rental car to be brought around and checked out of the hotel at noon. He decided to take a quick drive out to Tybee Island because it was too early to go to the library.

His brochure told him Tybee Island used to be called Savannah Beach. That was many years ago when a train ran from downtown to the island. Now there is no longer a train. It turned out to be a thirty-minute drive over several bridges and along picturesque salt marshes packed with wading birds. As he parked his rental car he noticed the sky darkening. He used his credit card to pay the parking meter and put the receipt on the dash of the car. Jock walked out on the long pier thinking about Australia and Grace and how she would love this.

He felt conspicuous on the beach wearing a white, long-sleeve Alexander McQueen sport shirt, navy Armani trousers and black Gucci loafers. Jock hadn't expected the temperature to be so warm nor the humidity so high. He appreciated the on-shore wind that made the walk

218

bearable. At the end of the pier he watched the Northern gannets dive like arrows into the choppy waters.

After the pier, he walked down to the beach thinking about Grace playing on the beach in Australia. He longed to see her.

The beach was actually pretty nice. It was obviously low tide because there was a long stretch of hard sand from the dunes down to the water. A flock of Black skimmers idled on the sand. The clouds were dark, and they seemed to be moving toward shore at a rapid pace.

Walking toward the water he thought about his choices in women, Laura, Sandra and Alexa. He sure had a talent for picking bitches.

Jock sensed Les knew he was after something valuable. *Les is in Jacksonville. I need to keep an eye out for him.*

He checked the time on his phone. He turned around and walked back to the parking lot. The wind picked up and it started to sprinkle. The skimmers rose in unison, a black and white cloud, and skimmed over the shallow choppy waves.

On the way back to Skidaway Island he had to use the windshield wipers intermittently. The radio said a tropical storm over the Atlantic had been named Erika by the National Weather Service. There was a slight chance that it could develop into a hurricane by the weekend. *But I'll be long gone,* he thought.

* * *

219

While Jock was taking in the local sights, Les had spent the last two days having some magnetic signs made to put on the doors of his truck. They advertised him to be the "Landscape Cop" and listed one of his burner phone numbers. He had attached the Comcast bar code to his driver's side window. Now he could enter the gated community whenever he needed to.

Parked across the street from the Hyatt, Les watched as Jock retrieved the red Ford Focus from the valet. The bell hop put two large suitcases in the trunk of the small car.

He's checked out, thought Les. He followed Jock as he drove away from the hotel onto Bay Street and proceeded east all the way to Tybee Island. Slouched down, he waited in the parking lot while Jock walked the beach. Les looked around, didn't see anyone else in the parking lot and covertly placed a tracking device under the rear bumper of Jock's rental car. It would tell Les where Jock went without Les having to be right on his tail.

When Jock returned to his car, Les stayed where he was for a while. He watched the screen on his monitor and saw that Jock was driving west along Highway 80. He pulled out and followed Jock at a distance. He stayed about a mile behind Jock all the way to Skidaway Island.

When Les began the long descent from the crest of the bridge over the Intracoastal Waterway, he could see Jock's car in the distance. It was approaching the second stop light and moved into the left turn lane. The first light after the bridge turned red and Les screeched to a halt. It was a good thing he had attached the tracker to Jock's car. Jock could be heading for the library or he could be going to Laura's house. Both were in that direction.

He was watching the GPS screen when someone behind him honked his horn. The light had turned green, but Les hadn't noticed. Powering down his window, he stuck out his arm and flipped the bird to the driver behind him.

Les turned left onto Lake Street. Jock's car had stopped in the block just past the pharmacy. Les drove on. As he passed, he noticed Jock sitting in the driver's seat.

CHAPTER 46

Laura's day gathered around her and she was able to keep her hair appointment with Stephan and make it to the Library by 2:30. Her shift moved agonizingly slowly. Merilee talked endlessly. It started to rain around 4 o'clock. The patrons today had come in sporadic busloads. Gratefully, she'd not had a second to sit idly with Merilee. Finally, at 4:35 Merilee found time to check through the stacks of books assigned to her.

"I'm off to check my stacks now," she cooed to Laura as three or four more people trickled in, all returning books.

"Please do." muttered Laura as she went about her checking-in duties.

Merilee decided she'd check from the lower shelf up to the top shelf. When she bent down to scan the lower shelf her back spasmed badly. She immediately raised her hand and grabbed the upper edge of the bookshelf, hauling herself to an upright position. Her hand missed the edge of the shelf and caught on a statue too near the edge. The thing fell off the shelf smack onto the floor.

"Oh lord," whispered Merilee, whose back pain went from surprisingly sharp to bearable as she righted herself. She carefully leaned back down and picked up the bronze statue of a child reading. It felt quite heavy for such a small piece of art. I hope I haven't broken this thing.

As Merilee stared at the statue, trying to ignore her back pain, she noticed the felt covering on the base of the stature had come partially unglued. Quickly glancing over her shoulder, Merilee saw Laura was still checking in books. Apparently, Laura had not even heard the noise. The rain poured down on the Library roof like an avalanche of rocks. The cacophony must have covered up the sound of the falling statue.

The dislodged felt covering on the statue's base intrigued Merilee. She peered into the small dark hollow. Her curiosity rewarded, she saw a velvety dark material. She pushed two fingers into the cavity and felt a soft crumpled soft bag with hard chunky objects within.

Merilee turned her injured back to the desk so no one would notice her fishing out the black velvet bag from the base of the statue. Taking one quick peek inside the drawstring bag, she almost dropped it in shock.

Oh, my Lord. She shoved the smallish bag into the voluminous side pocket of her couture trousers. In another heartbeat, Merilee smoothed out the felt and replaced the statue back on the bookshelf.

Merilee said rather too loudly to Laura, "Laura, honey. Do you mind if I leave early? I have to go home. My back went into spasm and the pain is just awful. I need to get home to lie down and take a pain pill. It's almost closing time and it's raining. No one will likely come in now. Do you mind closing by yourself?"

* * *

Les drove around the block and parked in front of Sun Trust Bank across the square from the library. From there he could see Jock's car and would be able to see if Jock got out.

Half an hour later Jock got out of his car and jogged across the street, through torrential rain and entered the library. Les started his truck, cruised slowly around the corner and parked in front of the office building nearer to the library. This position allowed him to see anyone entering or leaving the library so long as he kept his windshield wipers running.

*   *   *

Jock had no idea so many people would want to cram into the building. *This is going to be to my advantage.* People wandered up and down the aisles, peering at book spines, loudly discussing authors with the two volunteers. One of the volunteers was Laura, the "late" Tommy Petroff's dearly beloved, who'd bled him dry while they were married. His faked demise in China had freed him of her and her decidedly materialistic, keep-up-with-the-Joneses way of life. Jock had never missed her. Not one iota. And to top it off, the stupid woman had given away the bronze which housed his cache of several millions in cold, hard diamonds.

Laura looked up as Jock approached the desk. "May I help you?"

"Do you have today's New York Times?"

"No. We don't have periodicals." Looking at him she continued, "You remind me of someone. I just can't think who."

"I'm not sure where you could know me from unless you're Australian . . ." and he'd laughed as if making a huge joke, but praying the mint he'd spent on that plastic surgery was worth it. "I'll wander around and see what you have."

Over by the "A's" in the fiction section, Jock spotted the bronze. His bronze. His glittery future. He pretended to gaze at a book, then feigning surprise at seeing such artwork, he picked up the statue, hefted it in his hands and placed it back on the shelf because some old biddy was clearly going to knock into him if he didn't move. The statue's weight told him his affluent future was a cinch.

He slipped into the bathroom under cover of the crowd at the desk. Thank the gods for all these avid readers. He locked the door and settled down onto the toilet seat.

CHAPTER 47

Les watched people entering and leaving the library, but he didn't see Jock come out. Toward the five o'clock closing time, foot traffic slowed. The rain beat down harder. He checked his iPhone for the latest radar report. It showed a widening band of rain from west of Savannah out to about a hundred miles off shore. The center of circulation of Tropical Storm Erika was southeast of the Bahamas at 24° N and 74° W and moving NNW at fifteen mph with a likely landfall on Saturday somewhere between Daytona Beach, Florida and Wrightsville Beach, North Carolina. Having lived in the Jacksonville, Florida, area for many years, Les had become accustomed to watching the tracks of these tropical storms and hurricanes, especially in August and September.

Just before five o'clock Les saw a woman clutching a purse under her arm run out of the front door of the library. She dashed across the street. The lights on a blue Volvo flashed as she scrambled in. She started the car, turned on the windshield wipers full blast and drove away.

About ten minutes later, Les saw the lights go out in the library. Shortly after, another woman left the library by the door closest to him. She dashed through the rain to a silver Jaguar parked nearby. Although he couldn't be sure because of the heavy rain, the woman looked a lot like Laura. He continued his watch. Still no sign of Jock.

To his surprise he saw the silver Jaguar return and park directly in front of the library. The woman got out and splashed across the memorial bricks entering the library through the front door.

Les got out of his truck, pulled his rain jacket over his head and ran to the nearest door of the library. That was the door Laura, if it was Laura, exited when she left the building before. The door was locked but he could wait around the corner of the building. No one could see him, plus he was protected from the rain by the overhang of the roof.

* * *

He'd been closeted in that cupboard of a bathroom for over an hour now. Jock heard the other volunteer, what was her name, Merilee . . . or something perky with bells on it.

"Laura, honey. Do you mind if I leave early? I have to go home. My back went into spasm and the pain is just awful. I need to get home to lie down and take a pain pill. It's raining so no one will likely come in now."

"Of course, Merilee, go home now. No one is here and I'll start turning off lights as soon as you go. I'll take your name tag back to the office with mine."

Jock heard the front door opening. "Drive home safely, Laura, and say hello to Javier for me. That man is such a darling . . . he does beautiful bronzes. Just so divine."

Merilee couldn't wait to get home. She would have run barefoot all the way in the pouring rain if she had to. She couldn't wait to show Fredericka and Fournier what a

227

big surprise she accidentally discovered. And it was all hers. Wasn't possession nine tenths of the law?

Her little darlings were going to be wearing faux mink onesies and tennis bracelet collars if this was what she thought it was. Merilee Margaret, you have just scored big time. Merilee almost sang this to herself as she skipped inside from her garage. Paradoxically, no back pain at all.

The rain pelted down on the roof like a kinetic attack from Thor. Merilee remembered he was the Norse God of thunder, or was it lightning . . . whatever. Rain was rain. And Merilee, saturated after her sprint from the library front door to her car, didn't give a flying fig.

First thing, she let out the ferrets from their room, so they could ogle at her treasure trove. Next, she plopped down at the dining room table. She moved the elaborate centerpiece of life-like magnolias with branchy leaves floating in a bed of glass balls, all tastefully contained in her signed Kosta Boda bowl. Merilee shook out the contents of the tightly-packed, black velvet bag.

"My, my, my," Merilee sucked in her breath with a whistle. So unlike her to whistle. Only her babies were there to witness this event, no harm in being herself.

Three pairs of bright eyes peered at the sparkling pile of diamonds . . . pink, blue, white, and yellow prisms danced around the room. "I love it. They looked like Crown Jewels."

Fournier took a tentative swipe at a few diamonds on the periphery. Merilee gave him the glare and he backed up, swishing his tail. While Merilee focused on

Fournier, Fredericka silently patted one of the smoothly faceted baubles and quickly pawed it under her body, looking innocent.

This must be a huge fortune. She could redo the enclosed pool. Merilee had no idea how much this booty could amount to. But what if they're paste? They must be real. Why else would they be hidden? They had the cut and faceted quality of real diamonds and they gleamed like true diamonds but, hell, cubic zirconium did the same. She scooped up a handful and pressed her treasure to her heart. How lovely they'd look around her neck, on her fingers, on her ears, in her hair, on her gowns . . . or converted into filthy lucre.

But then again, what if they were blood diamonds? Hadn't she heard something about children mining these precious commodities? Oh, well. She hoped they fed them nourishing food and paid their mothers money for the children's education after they grew too big to mine.

The truth of her situation slapped her upside her head.

Merilee scooped up the diamonds and poured them back into the velvet bag.

She would call Javier tomorrow and fish around a bit. Of course, she wouldn't tell him what happened, but it was his sculpture after all and maybe he knew something.

Right now I've got to hide these. No way can I just leave them on the dining room table. Someone could rob the house. Somebody definitely lost these pretties, but no one's going to steal them from me.

229

I hope no one saw me and Laura wasn't suspicious when I left early. Did she believe me when I had the sudden back pain?

The grandfather clock in the foyer chimed. She realized she had to leave for her Canasta group at CarolAnn's. Right now. She felt like calling CarolAnn and cancelling, but something told her to go.

CarolAnn couldn't play Canasta if the game turned into a big hairy gorilla and bit her on the shoulder. The other two women didn't know a card from a card sharp. I can't bear to sit around with those gossipy witches tonight. But, on second thought, maybe I should. If I don't show up they might think something is wrong.

She managed to get herself over to CarolAnn's house that night for the usual Canasta game; however, she couldn't concentrate on her cards.

Her Patek Phillipe watch, a gift from her last philandering husband, read almost midnight when she scurried into her house from the garage. The rain had not let up at all.

She walked around the house, making sure all the windows and doors were locked up tight. After which, Merilee took the bag up to bed with her and stuffed it under her pillow. Stripped down to bare flesh, Merilee sighed a sigh of happiness and glee. Lying on her thousand count sheets was pure heaven. Her two furry friends, Fournier, Fredericka curled against her like hot, comforting heartbeats.

CHAPTER 48

Jock extinguished the light in the restroom. He sat in darkness waiting for the light that crept under the door to go out. Finally, it did. He heard faint noises as Laura moved through the building. Jock cracked the door and heard only silence.

When he heard the back door clunk loudly shut, Jock cautiously eased out of the bathroom. He made his way to the bronze statue.

Quick as a rat down a rope he snatched up the statue. He turned it upside-down and tore at the felt padding. He stuck his index and middle fingers inside the hollow of the statue. He pulled out a torn piece of black velvet cloth. He felt it more than saw it because darkness overwhelmed the library in between lightning strikes.

Jock screamed. His rage was liquid and black as boiling oil.

It took him all of a minute to calm down and try to figure this out. What had happened? Had Laura found them and taken them? She didn't seem like she'd made a big find before she left. Maybe the statue hadn't been heavier when he'd first picked it up. Maybe that creep Javier had found them years ago. So many possibilities. Jock cursed.

Blue-white lightning lit up the outside of the building. Jock stared with disbelief as Laura ran through the rain to front door of the library. He skittered down the hallway and pressed himself into an alcove beside a fake Ficus almost as tall as he.

Laura Banderas, Laura Banderas. You bitch. Not only did you marry that slime artist, now you've stolen my diamonds. His rage bubbled over.

*   *   *

When Laura left the Library at 5:10, rain continued to pour like the sky had turned upside down. Her Chanel suit would be ruined. She dashed out of the self-locking door of the Library and raced to her car. I should have left with Marilee. It wasn't raining this hard then.

Visibility was nearly zero. The sky raged dark as midnight. She fumbled getting into her Jaguar. The car purred to life and she started to drive home. That's when she remembered her iPad on the front desk. Damnation. Her suit ruined, her shoes soaked, and now she had to drive back to the pharmacy to get the library key. The pharmacy kept a key on a hook in a store room.

Damn. Laura remembered that she'd neglected to lock the front door after Merilee left. She would chance it. Maybe the front library door is still open. Oh, she wished this rain would just let up for a few minutes. With that thought, Laura pulled up in front of the library and turned off the motor. She fairly flew from her car to the front door, praying desperately as she grabbed the handle.

Eureka! It's open.

Once inside, she hurried over to the desk without turning on the lights. She snatched her iPad off the desk and hurried down the hall toward the back door. She almost walked past Jock without seeing him. At that moment, a flash of lightning illuminated the interior of the library. The ensuing thunder clap caused Laura to scream.

Jock stepped out of the shadows. Stunned, Laura tried to step away from him but he stepped with her and grabbed her arm.

"Stop! You're hurting me. Take my purse. Let me go. Don't hurt me."

"Laura!"

She knew that voice but not that face. "Tommy?" She knew.

Jock knew she knew.

Her mind spun in a crazy spiral. They'd never found his body at the bottom of that cliff. This man, even though she couldn't see him properly in the dark was Tommy. Tommy is not dead.

"I know who you are!" she stuttered, "What do you want?" She could feel the hairs on the back of her neck stand up and her blood ran cold.

The bastard smiled at her. "My lovely Laura. Tell daddy what you did with his diamonds or I'll have to exact a punishment." His voice lilted seductively as if he were whispering sweet nothings into her ear.

She felt danger rush over her skin. Laura knew he was evil, no two ways about it, and she was scared senseless. "Get out of my way or I'll call the police."

She panicked and pushed her iPad into his chest.

He laughed at her. "Where are my diamonds, you money-grubbing fashion plate?"

"I don't know what you're talking about." Laura didn't want to hear anything more from this psychopath.

She wanted to get the hell out of there, away from him. He towered over her like a looming black angel of death.

"Where are they? Where are my diamonds?"

"Tommy, I don't have any idea what you're talking about. I don't know anything about any diamonds. What happened to your face? Why are you holding that statue?"

"I want to know what you did with my diamonds." He held up the statue to show her the empty cavity in the bottom. "Where are they? What have you done with them?"

"The only diamond I have is the one you gave me when we were married." She flashed her hand bearing the diamond ring he had given her many years ago.

Jock felt the heft of the statue still cradled in his left hand.

In one fell swoop, he brought the bronze down on the side of her head with all his might. She stared at him for a second. He slammed the side of her head again and she dropped like a rock. He knelt down and felt for a pulse but couldn't find one. Jock backed up stepping away from the pooling blood. "Shit! What have I done? I've got to get out of here."

He put the statue on the bookshelf holding the rental books, wiped his bloody hands on his pants, and ran toward the back door of the library. Bursting out the back door, he ran through the rain to his car. His rental car sat across Lake Street and he reached it with a thundering heart and thunder booming overhead. The manual transmission skidded as he forced the car into a U-turn and sped toward the Diamond Causeway.

CHAPTER 49

Les was caught off guard when the door burst open. He saw Jock sprinting. Les scrambled back to his truck. He followed as Jock drove toward Savannah. The rain was coming so hard now that driving was almost impossible. There was no traffic on the road, Les had to slow down to less than ten miles an hour just to be able to see the road directly in front of him. He could barely see the tail lights of Jock's car rapidly accelerating away from him.

Jock righted the skid and plowed through the rain. He slammed his foot on the gas. The car swayed and veered on the road leading to the bridge. Just as he got control of the wheel, a deer bounded in front of him. He swerved, but his speed made the car tilt on two wheels onto the bridge. The rain acted as a lubricant.

Jock righted the car crossing the center line. In the next second a bridge repair machine appeared, huge and ominous, in front of him. He overreacted swinging the wheel with a lurch. The car slid sideways into the guard rail. The impact jerked Jock forward. The airbag inflated. The back end of the car lifted. It rose up in a slow motion. The vehicle flipped over the rail and fell into the Intracoastal. He had no time to think about anything. No life flashed before his eyes.

Les reached the bridge and saw Jock skid, hit a piece of construction equipment, and flip over the guard rail into the river. As he got closer, he pulled over and got out of his car. Looking over the guard rail, he couldn't see

Jock's car in the river. The tide must be high because the marsh was nearly under water. The wind still played havoc with visibility. A bolt of lightning struck one of the nearby power poles. There was an instantaneous crash of thunder. Illuminated by the lightning, Les thought he might have seen the top of the red car sink beneath the churning waves. He stood in the wind and rain and watched to see if Jock got out. After several minutes, Les walked back to his car. He started driving and didn't stop until he reached Jacksonville.

CHAPTER 50

When Jock regained consciousness, he felt the car slowly filling with water. He didn't remember the storm, the deer, or crashing into some piece of equipment on the bridge. His left leg ached. The crash had twisted and bent the steering wheel shaft and forced the turn signal lever into his left thigh. It hurt like hell.

It was black as pitch when he awoke. At first he didn't know where he was. He couldn't see anything. Hearing swooshing sounds, he realized he was under water. He had to get out. He pushed aside the air bag that had exploded on impact. Then he unbuckled the seat belt. The engine had stopped but the lights were still shining under the water. He felt the lever piercing his left thigh. Carefully, with great pain, he slid the driver's seat all the way back and shifted the position of his leg to the left. By doing so, he was able to free up his leg.

Water covered his ankles. I've got to get out. Now. Jock touched his thigh and felt warm blood everywhere.

He tried to lower the window. The button clicked but nothing happened. Without the engine running, the power windows were dead.

He tried to open the driver's side door but it had jammed. Awkwardly he climbed over the console into the front passenger seat. He used his feet to push on the door. The water pressure proved too great for him to get out. He continued to push like a crazy man on the door. He created a small opening, but that only allowed more water to pour into the car. He ripped the partially inflated air bag off the steering wheel, held tightly to the air bag and continued to use his legs on the door.

The cold water rose to his neck. Fear coursed through him. The pressure inside and outside began to equalize. With adrenaline-induced strength, he was able to force the door open far enough to squeeze out into the wet blackness.

He floated to the surface of the river by kicking and holding tight to the air bag using it as his makeshift life preserver. Below him the car's headlights dimmed and went out. In the darkness, he floated with the current. Blustery winds roiled the water. Sputtering and coughing water, he had no idea where he was or which way would lead him to land. Lightning flashed. In that instant he could see a small beach off to his right. Helped by a weak current, he half floated and half swam toward the beach. As he crawled up on the sand, he collapsed.

When he looked around he saw a boat ramp and a building in the distance but nothing much else except a large log half out of the water near him.

For a moment in the dim light cast by a sodium vapor lamp on a nearby pole, he thought he saw the log drift toward him. At first he thought the strong wind was moving the log. Jock blinked his eyes rapidly. The log had metamorphosed into a seven-foot gator. He limped and stumbled toward the small building. He got in and slammed the door overcome by the smell of urine. Thankfully the power was still on. He looked at his blood-soaked thigh. Ripping some cloth towels from the dispenser, Jock wrapped them tightly around his thigh and then passed out.

He woke and had no idea what time it was. That's when he saw daylight under the door. Cautiously opening the door, he looked for the alligator. No alligator.

He had to shield his eyes from the sun beating down on him from a cerulean sky. His leg hurt, but the bleeding had stopped.

I need some dry clothes.

Rising unsteadily, he began to open the door but stopped when he heard sirens. From where he stood he could see the Diamond Causeway and the bridge high above him. Police cars and vans were racing over the bridge toward Skidaway Island on the other side of the Intracoastal Waterway.

After he lost sight of them, he made his way across the parking lot and up the access road to the Causeway. He crossed over to the other side of the road. Shuffling toward Savannah, he stuck out his thumb.

Eventually, a man in a brown pickup pulled over and asked, "Hey buddy. You look like you could use a lift." He eyed the rag around Jock's thigh and asked, "Are you okay?" The driver stared at him.

The truck had oversize wheels. The cab looked to be ten feet off the ground. The man leaned over and pushed the door open. Using his last ounce of strength, Jock pulled himself up by the grab bar.

"Thanks mate. I've had a rough night. First my car broke down in the middle of the storm. I couldn't get a ride so I slept in the car. I need to get some dry clothes and find someone to tow my car. Do you have any ideas?"

"Well there is always Wally World."

"What's that?"

"Walmart. They're open this morning. You could get some new duds there. I could take you. First, I have to drop my dog off at the vet over on Eisenhower."

Jock turned around and looked in the pickup truck bed to see a huge black Rottweiler, slobbering and wagging his tail.

"Thanks, but just a gas station with a phone would be great." The driver gave Jock a handful of quarters.

Jock had lost his phones in the crash. The only things he salvaged were his waterlogged passport, plastic driver's license, and credit cards.

The plan had never been to fly back to Australia. He knew there was no way he could get past customs with the diamonds. Instead, he had arranged to travel back to Australia on Captain Panama's ship 'The Wayward Wind', berthed at the Garden City Terminal on the Savannah River. Once on board he could dry out his Passport.

The old man dropped Jock off at the Enmarket on Waters Avenue. "Take care of that leg mister."

Enmarket was a convenience store with gas pumps. Entering the store, it felt as if he were walking into a freezer. The temperature outside felt scorching even at 9 o'clock in the morning. The humidity made it feel even warmer. The temperature in the store must have been about sixty. His damp clothes caused Jock shiver uncontrollably. He asked the cashier if they had a pay phone.

She pointed outside. "It's next to the Ice Machine, but I don't know if it works."

People bought Jerky, soft drinks in massive two liter containers, plastic wrapped sandwiches, and bags of chips, and cigarettes by the carton.

Jock stepped out of the store and back into the warmth. Most people going in and coming out were dressed as if they were going to work, but not office work. More like work cutting grass, fixing plumbing, putting on a new roof or installing cable. None of these people noticed his clothes or the makeshift bandage tied around his leg. They were too busy purchasing the necessities required to start their work day.

After finding the pay phone, Jock called and Panama answered. "Hey, Panama, it's me, Jock MacInty. I'm ready to go back to Oz."

"No problem. We leave port in sixteen hours."

Jock told him he'd be at the McDonalds on Waters.

"I'll send transport. Be ready." Panama broke off the connection.

Jock slowly headed toward McDonalds half a block up the road. Once inside, he ordered an egg McMuffin, fries and a large coffee. He hadn't eaten for about twenty-four hours. The food tasted like ambrosia.

CHAPTER 51

An hour later, Jock, on his fourth coffee refill, looked out the window. He saw a white pickup truck with "Georgia Ports Authority" printed on the side. His ride.

"Hey man. My name's Bobby Joe. Are you Jock?"

Jock didn't know if his last name was Joe or if that was part of his first name. It didn't matter. Bobby Joe was a twenty something year old kid with red hair. He looked as if he hadn't shaved in a few days and smelled as if he hadn't showered for a week. Bobby Joe told Jock his job at the Garden City Terminal was moving containers from the ships to the trucks that would carry them almost anywhere in the southeast part of the country.

For the next forty minutes Bobby Joe nattered on about his work and his pay, which Bobby Joe thought was good.

As they got closer to the port, they entered Garden City. Jock thought the name fit this arm pit of a town as well as the Garden State fitted New Jersey. But what did he care? He wasn't going to live here. The important thing was his ship had come in and he would soon be leaving.

Bobby Joe pulled the truck up to the security checkpoint. The guard looked at Jock and glanced into the truck bed. He passed them through without any delay. They drove through acres and acres of containers, stacked six high. A canyon with walls made of steel containers. They passed large machines lifting containers off the stacks and hauling them down marked lanes. The machines maneuvered the loads quickly. The containers were bigger than the pickup truck and Bobby Joe had to be careful not to be crushed.

Jock didn't see any ships. Eventually they turned right down another row of containers and he saw a ship parked alongside a dock. Enormous cranes moved containers from the shore to the ship. Jock had not expected such a massive ship, one that looked like a rust bucket. The faded black hull competed with streaks of rust.

Bobby Joe left Jock at the bottom of a steep metal stairway leading up the side of the 'Wayward Wind.' "Thanks for the lift," yelled Jock. He didn't know if Bobby Joe could hear him with all of the noise.

After the truck pulled away, Jock grabbed the hand rail and began to climb the stairs. He didn't count the steps but he must have climbed at least five stories until he got to the main deck. Exhausted from his climb, he hoped that they had a doctor on board so he could get some relief from the pain.

Once on deck, he was greeted by a seaman who seemed to be old enough to have traveled with Captain Cook. The short man wore an oil-stained gray jumpsuit with a red kerchief tied around his head, sweating and cussing like a pirate.

"Follow me. I'm to take you to the bridge to see my Cap'n," said the old geezer.

Meeting the captain entailed climbing up another series of stairs or, as old guy called them, ladders. Ladders were a good name because they were much steeper than

243

any staircase Jock had ever encountered. By the time they reached the companionway leading to the bridge, his leg throbbed. He could see he was now almost as high as the top of the enormous cranes still busily loading containers onto the ship.

When he entered the hatch into the bridge he saw Captain Panama holding a clip board. Between his teeth bobbled an unlit but almost completely smoked cigar and he was barking orders into his walkie-talkie.

The Captain turned as the hatch snapped shut and noticed Jock. "Jock. My man. It's good to see you. Welcome aboard. I'm putting you in the owner's cabin. It's not much but it's better than bunking with the crew."

"Hi, Cap. You don't know what I've gone through to get here. Do you have a doctor on board?"

"Ha! Ha! Ha! You're joking, right? You think this is the Queen Elizabeth? No doctor. But we got a medic." Panama's eyes dropped to Jock's bandaged bleeding leg.

"I had a car accident last night and hurt my leg. Can your medic could take a look. I might need stitches because it's bleeding again. At least maybe he could give me something for pain."

"Sure. Sure. Stormy, take Mr. MacInty down to medical bay. After that show him his cabin," the captain said to the old guy who had brought Jock up to the bridge. "Where are your bags?" Panama asked.

"No bags. Just me."

"OK. After you unpack, ha, ha, ha, come on back up here. We should be finished loading the cargo by 16:00 hours. The paperwork will take another hour then we'll head over to the Gentlemen's Club for drinks and some titty viewing. It's the best place from here to the Canal. We leave on the tide at 22:30."

"There's a tide? I thought this was a river," said Jock.

"Sure, there's tide. It comes right up the river. The next high tide today will be 7.3 feet at 22:00 tonight. It'll float us out to the ocean."

"Then where?" asked Jock.

"Well, first port of call is Cartagena, Columbia, to drop off some containers and pick others up. After that it's on to the Panama Canal. My ship will fit through the old locks. We stop for fuel at the Port of Balboa, Panama, on the Pacific side. From there it's west across the Pacific to Auckland, New Zealand, where we drop off more containers and pick some up. The end of the line will be Sydney about thirty-one days from now if we have good weather," said Captain Panama.

Stormy took Jock down to the medical bay. It was small, only one stretcher, a shower and a few cabinets for medicine and instruments.

"When will the medic be here?" asked Jock.

"I'm the medic. I'm also the chief officer. There are only thirteen crew on this vessel, so we all double or triple up on jobs. Now, let's get a gander at that leg," said Stormy.

Jock sat down and pulled down his pants. "Oh, this don't look good. Could be infected because that's a deep gash. I'll sew it up and give you a shot of antibiotic."

Afterwards, Stormy took Jock to his cabin, neat but small, smaller than a cheap motel room. It held a single bed, a table and a chair. He asked Stormy if he had a hair dryer on board.

"Your hair looks good mate. The cook's got a blower. He uses it to dry the armpits on his t-shirt."

Later, Jock and Captain Panama were at the bar at the gentleman's club. Half naked women danced on the bar almost on top of them. Another woman bumped on a small stage gyrating around a center pole. The place was as bad as Jock had imagined. Although smoking inside bars had been banned in Savannah for years, the club still stunk of stale cigarette smoke and spilled beer. The lighting came from neon beer signs hung on the walls and from the ceiling. The floor felt sticky. The red vinyl seats on the bar stools were torn and cracked.

Panama was on his fourth scotch when Jock asked him, "Is the 'Wayward Wind' one of Chu's boats?"

"Ship, lad! Ship! She's hardly a boat. My ship is nearly a thousand feet in length and can carry 5,000 TEUs. TEU stands for Twenty foot Equivalent Unit. Most of our containers are forty feet long so each one counts as two TEUs. Most are eight feet wide and eight and half feet high. She was built by Hyundai Heavy Industries in South Korea in 1985 and sold to Hapag-Lloyd out of Germany. Chu bought her in 2011. She spent a year in dry-dock at the Okpo shipyards in South Korea being retrofitted. She's a gem, ain't she?

"Well, she looks like she's seen a lot of action," said Jock. He wasn't going to say it, but he thought to himself she looked like she'd been ridden hard and put away wet. *I hope this boat will make it to Australia.* "Are his other ships like this one?"

"What other ships?" asked Panama.

"Chu told me he planned to purchase a dozen ships and retrofit them," said Jock.

"I don't know about that. The 'Wayward Wind' is the only ship he owns," said Panama.

CHAPTER 52

THURSDAY, AUGUST 6, 2015

Dash drove his white Toyota Prius security car up to the front of the library and screeched to a halt behind a silver Jaguar. The strobe on his car flashed green. The rain and wind of yesterday were a memory. Today a robin's egg blue painted the sky. Tropical Storm Erika had been downgraded to a tropical depression leaving no threat to Savannah or the east coast. Dash threw open the library door at exactly 9:43, only seven minutes after security received the frantic call. The woman caller reported someone injured.

When he entered the library, Molly Cohen was slumped in a chair at the desk. She looked pale and her hands trembled.

"Molly, I didn't know that you were the one who called security."

"I think I know who it is," Molly said without preamble.

Dash covered Molly's hand with his. "Dash, it's terrible. Come." She stood, turned, and her steps faltered as she moved toward the hall leading to the new wing.

When Dash saw the body on the floor and the floor covered with blood he asked Molly, "Did you touch her? Or feel for a pulse?"

"Yes. She's dead," Molly said quietly.

"Go back to the desk. Please."

Dash pulled out his cell phone and dialed his friend, Conor Donovan. In a firm, calm voice he said,

"Conor, it's Dash. We have a situation here. It's a possible homicide at the Village Library on Skidaway Island. You better get here and bring your crime scene guys and a coroner. I'm at the scene and I'll keep it secure until you get here." Dash ended the call and walked to the front door and locked it. Then he went back to the body and brushed Molly's shoulder with his hand.

Molly glanced at her phone and it showed 10:00. The library should be opening now. Jane should be here by now. Molly took a sheet of paper from the front desk. She printed the word "CLOSED" on the paper and taped it to the front door of the library. She stayed by the door so she could let the police in when they arrived. She had to open the door and assure a few patrons the library would be open tomorrow. She told them all fines would be forgiven today.

Molly heard sirens. A Savannah Chatham police car sped up to the front of the library. A uniformed officer got out of the car, adjusted his side arm, and approached the door. Before he reached the door, a plain black car pulled up with blue and white lights flashing behind the front grill.

Conor Donovan, dressed in a navy sport coat, khaki pants, white shirt, and striped tie exited from his unmarked and caught up with the police officer. Molly unlocked the door and let them in.

Dash nodded to Conor.

Conor said, "I pity the people who have to drive into town from Skidaway. The traffic was a parking lot on Diamond Causeway."

"What was it this time?" asked Dash.

"Apparently a car went off the bridge last night in the storm. One lane is closed. They pulled a car out, but no driver. Divers are searching the river now," Conor said. Conor turned toward the uniformed officer and said, "Put crime scene tape up in front of the library, take a walk around the outside of the building to see if anything is amiss."

A police crime scene van and a medical examiner's wagon joined the other vehicles in front of the library, thus making it impossible for any cars to use the street in front of the library. With the usual morbid curiosity, people gathered in the park across from the library.

Dash and Conor took the crime scene team back to the hall where the body remained on the floor amid a pool of blood. The medical examiner knelt down next to the body and without flourish pronounced her dead at the scene.

Conor asked, "Can you give me a time of death?"

The ME said, "She's been dead at least twelve hours and perhaps as many as twenty-four. I'll know more when I get her on the slab."

"What about a cause of death?" Conor asked.

"I don't have my X-ray glasses on, but it looks like blunt force trauma. My first clue is the large gash on her head where all of the blood seems to have originated. I'll let you know when I autopsy."

A photographer walked around the body taking pictures of the scene. She photographed the trail of bloody foot prints leading into a large room at the end of the hall, through the office and out the back door. She took pictures of a statue resting on top of a book shelf in the main area just outside the hall. The statue appeared to be covered with blood.

Conor looked around the immediate area of the body while the ME and his crew prepared to remove it. One of the assistants almost slipped in the blood as they lifted the body onto the stretcher. Conor noticed a ring on the dead woman's finger. It caught his eye because he had never seen a stone that size.

After the ME and his crew left with the body, Dash once again locked the front door of the library. "Sit down." he told Molly. She still looked shaken.

Conor and Dash each took a chair in front of Molly. Conor pulled out a small spiral bound pad from the inside pocket of his sport coat. He shrugged off his jacked and hung it on the back of the chair.

"Are you up to answering some questions?" asked Conor.

"Of course." Molly said.

"Did you find the body?"

"Yes."

"When?"

"I got here about 9:30 and was just turning on the lights when I nearly stumbled over her."

"Was anyone with you Molly?"

"No. My co-worker doesn't usually show up until right before we open at 10. And today she didn't show. Thank God."

"Did you touch anything?"

"I felt for a pulse, but she was dead. I must have brushed against that statue on the shelf near the window. There is a lot of blood on it. That's why I've got blood on my blouse."

"Do you know who the woman is?"

"I'm not sure, but I think it is Laura Banderas, a volunteer here. Or at least she was a volunteer here."

The questioning continued for several hours. Conor and Dash took notes. Molly showed them the schedule for the previous day and they saw Laura Banderas was scheduled to work the last shift ending at 5 PM with a woman named Merilee MacKenzie. They found Merilee's number and address in the volunteer directory.

Dash told Conor there appeared to be bloody footprints leading from the body in the hall to the back door of the library. The footprints were too large to have been made by Molly. "These prints look to have been made by a man or a very large woman.

Conor told the CSI tech, "Be sure to bag that statue. Did you find her ID?"

"Not yet." said the tech.

"What about that silver Jag out front?" said Dash.

"Let's go take a look." said Conor.

Dash tried the passenger door and found it unlocked. "We got a hand bag here." said Dash stepping aside.

Conor reached in and picked up the hand bag, glanced at the back seat and found it empty. They took the handbag into the library. Conor placed it on the desk,

looked in the bag, saw a wallet, and pulled it out. He saw
a Georgia Driver's License . . . Laura Banderas.

CHAPTER 53

"When will we be able to reopen the library? Molly asked walking toward them.

"We'll let you know. Probably several days until we complete our crime scene investigation."

"I need to call the library president. I have to tell her what happened."

"I'd like you to wait on that call until after I have had a chance to talk to her." said Conor. "I think we're finished for now, Molly. Do you need a lift home? One of my officers can take you."

"No. I'm fine."

"I'll need your key to lock up here when we're finished," Conor continued.

"I don't have a key. We usually pick up the key at the pharmacy to open the library, but when I got here this morning I found the door unlocked. We lock the front door from the inside and exit out the self-locking back door. Call Sue Sturges, the president. She has an extra key. Let me write her number down for you."

Dash walked Molly to the door, unlocked it, and gave her a peck on her cheek. "I'll come by later."

After Molly left, Dash and Conor went over the crime scene again. This time with greater care. "It doesn't look like it was a robbery. There is cash in the drawer, an iPad on the floor and of course that diamond ring on her finger. A thief would have definitely taken the cash, the ring, and probably the iPad. I'm finished for now. I'm going to go and speak with Mr. Banderas,"

Conor said as he stood and threw his jacket over his shoulder.

"Is there anything I can do?" asked Dash.

"Well, you really have no official position, but I suppose there is nothing wrong with you asking some questions in your capacity as Chief of Security. Why don't you call Sue Sturges and get a key for the library. You could call Merilee MacKenzie too and find out when we can meet with her. I need to talk to Merilee MacKenzie and see what she knows. She may have been the last person to see Laura Banderas. Aside from the murderer, that is." Conor said. I'm going downtown for the post-mortem. Let's get together again Saturday at the Village Bar and Grill about 7. Bring Molly and I'll bring Meg.

"I'll drive over to the house of the library president and get the key and ask her what she might know about the victim and when she last saw her. I'll see you on Saturday."

                    *   *   *

A tall woman in tennis attire opened the front door. "Yes, can I help you?"

"Mrs. Sturges?"

"Yes." she noticed the Landings Security car and asked, "And you are?"

"My name is Donato Santorelli. I'm the Chief of Security for The Landings. I need to ask you some questions."

"About what?" I was just getting ready to leave for tennis. I can spare a few minutes. That's all."

"I'm sorry to inform you there has been a serious incident at the Village Library. I understand you are the library president."

"Yes, I am." Sue Sturges gasped. "What happened?"

"A woman was found dead in the library hall this morning. She has not been positively identified, but she may have been one of your volunteers."

"Oh, my God. No."

"The police are treating it as a possible homicide. When was the last time you were at the library?"

"Let me think. I go there whenever someone calls and I have a regular shift on Monday. But, I think Monday was the last time I was there this week."

Dash took out a small note pad and a pen from his pocket. "Does the library have security cameras? I didn't see any when I looked around."

"No. We have a very small budget. We don't keep much cash on hand and there is nothing to steal except books."

"Do you know a Laura Banderas?"

"Is it Laura?"

"It's still uncertain."

"She's been one of our volunteers for many years and a generous supporter of the library."

"What do you mean by supporter?"

"She made a substantial contribution when we were raising funds to expand a few years ago. She usually makes a donation at the end of each year. And recently she gave us a very nice bronze statue sculpted by her husband, Javier Banderas, a very noted artist."

"What kind of statue?"

"It is a small sculpture of a child reading a book. It is on a book shelf near the rear window."

"When was the last time you saw Mrs. Banderas?"

"Not since last month when I happened to go to the library while she was working."

"I'm afraid that you will not be able to reopen the library until we have finished our investigation. That may be several days. I was told that you have a key to the library. We would like to borrow it until we are finished."

"Yes. If you wait here I'll go get it." Sue turned and went back into the house. When she returned, she gave the key to Dash and said, "I'll need to inform our volunteers the library will be closed until further notice."

Dash thanked her and left with the key.

As she closed the door she thought, I must remember to reprogram the computer system so people with books coming due will not be charged fines or rental fees while we are closed.

CHAPTER 54

Merilee bolted awake to the phone ringing off the hook. She glanced at the clock. Oh, my god. It's already noon. Half the day is gone. Time to get up. She stumbled to the phone.

"Merilee, Merilee, did you hear yet? Your friend, Laura, the one who works at the library with you. She's dead and the police are all over the library like white on rice. They had to close today. That's how we found out. Library closed and all these flashing lights with Security cars up the yin yang." A fast blur of words.

"CarolAnn, is that you?" whispered Merilee into the phone. She couldn't say anything else because her throat felt drier than the Gobi Desert at midday in August.

"Of course it's me. Did you hear what I said?" CarolAnn, her neighbor up four houses, couldn't stop babbling with information. "The woman is deader than a doornail and to top that, someone went over the bridge last night in the storm. Ran into the bridge repair equipment and flipped over the rails dead square into the Intracoastal."

"Noooo," whispered Merilee as she fished the velvet bag of shiny baubles out from under her pillow.

"Yes," CarolAnn rushed on. "Since you worked yesterday, you know they're gonna come and ask you questions because you were the last person to see Laura alive." A brief pause as CarolAnn took a breath in. "You did work yesterday afternoon at the library with your friend Laura didn't you?"

Merilee felt two drops of icy sweat bead under her arms and slide down her sides like moving glaciers. Her hands started shaking badly and she plopped her bare bottom back on top of the bed. "What happened?" she managed to force out of her closed throat.

"Apparently someone bashed in her head and Molly Cohen found the body at the crack of dawn this morning. I suppose it was 9:30 when she got to the library, right?" CarolAnn sucked in another quick breath before continuing. "That's why I never volunteer to do the first library shift. It's much too early and you just never know what you're going to find when you get there. And this is much worse than when the dog got munched by that big gator a few years back. Some golfer in his golf cart saw part of the dog's body floating in the lagoon over near Bartram somewhere."

"And you remember that time Don found the snake up in the ceiling when he was fixing the air conditioning? I mean, what a surprise! Can you imagine being Molly Cohen, who happens to be a doctor, thank the gods for small mercies, because apparently she didn't panic. I woulda panicked for sure. I don't think I've ever seen a dead body. And you know, Merilee, I think Molly Cohen knew Laura too . . . from some place up north . . . one of those ritzy suburbs in Connecticut . . . Greenwich, I think. Course I could be wrong."

All Merilee could manage, "Really . . ."

"And, you know, someone told me Molly Cohen's husband died under mysterious circumstances. Makes ya wonder, right? I mean, if the girl's a doctor she knows all the right ways to knock someone off and make it look like natural causes. But I don't think she bashed in Laura's head. Do you? You'd have to have a strong stomach for that. Yeah, and I've met Molly Cohen a few times at the hospital fund raisers. She seemed quite down to earth, not the type to do in her husband. I mean, after all, don't doctors take the Hippocratic Oath and all that? Do no harm blah, blah?"

Merilee dressed one-handed, donning linen pants and silk top vaguely matching. Her other hand had the phone grafted to her ear with CarolAnn's hot moist breath blowing all over her inner ear. It's amazing how fear can make you feel something you know is not there.

Fournier and Fredericka gathered and swirled around her ankles sniffing wildly probably smelling Merilee's fear oozing out of her pores as if someone had squeezed her.

"CarolAnn, I have to go, honey. I'll call you back later. Get more juice for me, okay?"

The phone was slick with sweat. She threw the receiver onto the bed and clutched the diamonds close to her breasts.

What to do! What to do!

Merilee hot-footed it downstairs followed by the furry gang. She stared around vacantly, desperately trying to think of a place to hide her find. Could her diamonds be connected to the current library drama? There has to be a connection.

At first she put them in a baggie, then into the ice bucket in the fridge freezer. Then she thought, that's the very first place someone searching for diamonds would look. Out of the freezer came the diamonds. She shoved them into one of a pair of her Manolo Blanhiks with the trademark red sole. Five minutes later, she retrieved the bag and sat down at the dining room table, still shaking from the phone conversation.

She jumped as the kitchen phone loudly reverberated. Her hands trembled violently when she tried to shove the bag behind the magnolia centerpiece. As Merilee got up to answer the phone, she saw her best hiding place - in plain sight - right in front of her.

"Ms. MacKenzie?" said a mellifluous deep voice.

"Yes . . . ?" Merilee answered hesitantly, "Who is this?"

"Sorry m'am, err . . . Ms. MacKenzie. This is Dash Santorelli, head of Landings Security. We were wondering if we could come over to talk to you for a bit. We have an issue at the library. We hope you can help us out."

"Oh. Well. Sure. What's happened at the library?" ventured Merilee now balancing the phone between her shoulder and her cheek. "When do you want to come over?"

"We could come over in about ten minutes if that's alright with you, Ms. MacKenzie . . ."

"Oh, can you give me a few more minutes? I'm just eating . . ." Merilee thought about the time. " . . . my lunch."

Dash told her fine and Merilee took her finger to the phone, clicking off.

She began desperately snatching all the magnolias and leaves out of the centerpiece on the dining room table. She lifted up the huge Kosta Boda crystal bowl and let the clear marble sized glass balls spill onto the table, corralled by dinner mats. She dumped the contents of her black velvet bag into the bowl, scooped back in the glass balls, swirled the mix together with her fingers then deftly placed the magnolias with artistic branches and huge leaves back into an arrangement.

The centerpiece looked perfect as if arranged by an expert. That was Merilee, she was the expert. Merilee smiled. In the kitchen she cut up the smallish velvet bag into very small pieces with her garden scissors. Then she slipped into outdoor flats and ran out to the backyard where a Bluebird box stood in the middle of the grass, removed from trees and whatnot, but protected by a baffle on the pole. She opened up the Bluebird box. Luckily the Bluebird had just started making another nest and no one was home. She sprinkled the handful of black velvet pieces into box. There, she told herself, a lovely nesting material for my birds.

CHAPTER 55

SATURDAY, AUGUST 8, 2015

Conor Donovan had been busy since Thursday, meeting with the Medical Examiner, the crime scene team, and interviewing people. He was late picking up Meg.

When Conor and Meg arrived at the Village Bar and Grill, Molly and Dash were already seated at a table near the front window. Dash had a long neck beer in front of him and Molly sipped unsweet tea. A young waitress put menus on the table.

Dash stood up while Meg seated herself.

"Sorry we're late."

"Hi," Molly said.

"Hi, Molly. Have you recovered from the terrible events of Thursday?" Meg asked.

"I think so, but I can't forget all that blood on the library floor," Molly answered.

"You look lovely tonight. Dash is a lucky guy," said Conor as he turned and called the waitress back to the table. "My wife will have a sweet tea. Right Meg?" She nodded assent. "I'll have a Beefeater martini, very dry, on the rocks, with a twist." The waitress said she didn't know if they had Beefeater, but she would check.

"How's the investigation going?" asked Dash.

Conor waited until the waitress was out of ear shot and said. "I met with Javier Banderas yesterday. He's a strange guy. He came downtown and formally identified his wife's body. But he didn't seem very upset about her death. He also identified the ring she was wearing as belonging to her. He seemed more interested in when he would be able to take possession of the ring than the investigation into his wife's murder."

Dash spoke up, "Sue Sturges, the president of the library, gave me this key." He stood, fished in his pants pocket and handed the key to Conor. "I asked her if the library has video cameras. She told me no because the cost would be prohibitive for such a small operation. There really isn't much to steal except books. But I was thinking maybe the Merrill Lynch office building next door might have some kind of surveillance. The Landings has surveillance cameras, but none are focused on the library. The closest is at the intersection of Lake Street and Diamond Causeway."

Dash looked at Conor and continued, "When I picked up the library key from the president, she told me the sculpture which might be the murder weapon had been donated to the library by the victim. The artist who created the statue was none other than her husband, Javier Banderas. Quite a strange coincidence if you ask me."

"I don't believe in coincidences," said Conor. "I think I'll interview Mr. Banderas again. I also talked to Merilee MacKenzie. She acted very nervous and she was as skittish as a cat. She didn't make eye contact with me when I questioned her."

"That's nothing new. She never looks at the person speaking to her," Molly said.

"It doesn't sound like you and Merilee are BFFs," Meg said.

"Definitely not. I've worked with her a few times at the library. She's not my cup of tea," Molly said.

Conor continued, "Marilee said she worked with Laura Banderas Wednesday afternoon at the library. She said she left the library before Laura a little before 5 o'clock. As far as she knows, Laura was the only person left in the building. That means whoever killed Laura was in the building when Merilee left, or that he or she came in later. It also means Laura was killed sometime between 5 on Wednesday and when Molly discovered the body Thursday morning. He glanced around to see if anyone seemed to be paying inordinate attention to them. He spotted the waitress returning and leaned across the table. In a low voice, "Let's keep this hush, hush."

The waitress came back with two drinks. She set Meg's sweet tea on the table.

When she placed Conor's drink down on a napkin. Conor took one look at it and said, "This is not what I ordered."

The waitress responded, "Our bartender said we don't have any Beefeater. All we have is Dewars or Johnnie Walker, so this is a Johnnie Walker martini."

"My dear," said Conor in a soft tone, "Johnnie Walker and Dewars are brands of Scotch. Scotch is brown like this drink you served. Beefeater is a brand of gin. Gin is clear. Ask the bartender if you have any gin."

The waitress picked up his drink, spilling some on the table. "Sorry. I'll be right back," she said, hoping she could salvage her tip.

"I wonder what she'll bring next," said Conor.

"She must be new. And, judging from the purple hair she's probably a student at the Savannah College of Art and Design," Dash commented with a slight grin.

"Dash! You're supposed to be a detective. You know very well that all of the students at SCAD don't have purple hair and all people with purple hair don't attend SCAD," Molly admonished.

"Sorry. I know. It was just a bad joke." Dash took a swallow of his beer.

Just then the waitress delivered Conor's second martini. At least it was the right color this time. He took a sip and smiled.

As she turned to leave, the waitress rolled her eyes.

"I'll check with Merrill Lynch about their security system," Conor said.

"Is Banderas a suspect?" asked Dash.

"At this stage everyone is a suspect, but we should be able to narrow it down once those bloody prints on the stature are analyzed."

CHAPTER 56

AT SEA

MONDAY, AUGUST 18, 2015

D espite Laura's recognizing him, he still felt more like Jock MacInty than the old Tommy Petroff.

He had never been on a ship before. Sure, he'd been on smaller crafts, sea-faring pleasure boats, but that was it. This huge pile of rust didn't fit the bill for a pleasure craft. His cabin had noisy, rusting pipes and peeling paint, the bunk hard and unforgiving as a bed of nails.

Jock spent his days out of the claustrophobic cabin. Mostly, he stared over the railing at the always changing sea. The Gulf of Mexico had been pitted with oil rigs, a surprise for Jock. He'd always thought of the Gulf of Mexico as a pristine, untouched stretch of bay.

On the fifth day out, the Wandering Wind docked in Cartagena, Columbia. Maybe Panama would let Jock off this rust bucket for a few minutes, let him lose his bloody sea legs, and get a feel for terra firma. He watched with fascination as the tug boats pushed the Wandering Wind against the dock. Shouts, whistles and yells echoed up and down the dock. The sounds of roaring motors, welding, grinding, and sliding metal against metal bombarded his ears. Christ, he had no idea how noisy these shipyards were.

"No offshore today, me hearty," snapped Panama as he walked down the deck towards Jock. It was as if he'd read Jock's thoughts. "Be better if ya stay in yer cabin. We be quick here. Snake quick."

God. He sounded like Captain Blackbeard. He knew an order when he heard one. Jock turned about face, headed down the deck and around a container, out of eyesight of Panama. There he stopped and waited until he heard Panama yakking on and descending the rough, gridded boardwalk down to the dock below. Panama was not quite morbidly obese because he still had muscle but it took time for him to maneuver down the scarred wooden walkway.

Jock stood next to the rail on the ship's deck. The port of Cartagena was loud. Men were shouting, bells ringing, whistles blasting, and motors roared. After a bit, he sneaked a glance over the railing. Panama was practically right below him, standing next to one leg of a massive blue crane. Each leg of the crane rose to a platform higher than the containers stacked on the ship's decks. The platform held a control booth where an operator controlled a long boom extended horizontally over the ship. The sheer magnitude of size put him in awe.

Attached to the boom by cables, a metal device efficiently clamped onto one the containers on board. It lifted the container and placed it on a decrepit looking truck on the dock below. The crane rode on steel rails and moved along the ship to select specific containers. As soon as the container was loaded onto the truck the truck drove away and another took its place.

Still partially hidden behind the rail, Jock watched five containers unloaded in this manner. After the unloading, the process was reversed. Trucks pulled up on the dock. The boom lowered, clamped onto the container, lifted it off the truck, raised it to just below the boom, moved it to the end of the boom and lowered it to the ship.

After three new containers were loaded on board, the activity slowed. It had started to get dark. Every few minutes more high-intensity dock lights flicked on. Reluctantly, Jock thought about returning to his cramped cabin.

As he was about to turn away, a sleek, black Mercedes limo slowly cruised up the dock. The limo slid to a halt a few feet past Panama. The front door opened and no interior lights came on as a tall figure stepped out and opened the back door for the passenger. A big wig, thought Jock.

Panama guardedly approached the black limo. Jock squinted down at the scene. Instantly he realized who the limo passenger was. Jock stepped back away from the railing. His heart started galloping in his chest.

The bloody man is Chu Wei, the same bastard who tried to scam another five mill out of me. Chu walked up to Panama and they stood talking, as another dark sedan slowly rolled out onto the dock and parked silently behind Chu's Mercedes. Two men dressed in black exited the

269

sedan and joined Panama and Chu Wei. All four men turned to watch as another semi-trailer carrying an orange container maneuver under the crane. Jock noted the orange container had no visible markings. All of the other containers on the Wayward Wind had shipping company names displayed all over them. Hanjin. Hapag-Lloyd. Maersk.

Two pickup trucks pulled up behind the semi-trailer on the dock. Each pickup had two men in the truck bed carrying what looked to be automatic assault rifles. The pickup drivers and passengers got out. The guys in the truck beds jumped lithely down. All eight men circled the semi holding the orange container. To Jock, it looked like these guys were ready to repulse any attack.

Chu, Panama, and the two men dressed in black, the sedan driver and passenger, strode purposefully to the semi with the orange container. One of the guys from the sedan climbed up metal steps and unlocked the doors of the container. Panama, Chu and the two players from the sedan stepped into the orange container on the semi.

What the hell were they all doing in that container? Curiosity overtook his hesitancy. Jock leaned over the railing.

After a few minutes, all four men reappeared from within the container and three descended the steps. The remaining guy clanged shut and locked the doors.

Chu walked briskly to his Mercedes with Panama struggling to keep up. Panama opened the car trunk, leaned in and retrieved a medium-sized aluminum clad suit case. Because Panama moved slowly, Chu grabbed it out of his hands and swung the case onto the hood with a dull thud.

Chu opened up the metal case with a flourish. Jock could almost hear the snap of the lock. The player from the dark sedan plunged his hand into the case and pulled out a stack of vacuum sealed bills. He produced a switch blade and deftly sliced open the wrapping. He fanned the bills, after which he put the bills back in the case, snapped it shut and handed it over to his driver who placed it in the sedan's trunk.

Panama spoke into a walkie-talkie which he pulled from his pocket. The crane lowered its giant clamp onto the orange container and swung it up over and onto the Wandering Wind's deck at the opposite end of the ship.

As soon as the orange container was on the ship, the eight-man army with their automatic assault rifles disbanded into their pick-ups. They followed the semi-trailer out of the ship yard as did the dark sedan. As Jock continued to watch, Chu glanced up. Jock merged into the shadows. Almost as quickly, Chu turned away and climbed into the back of his Mercedes Limo. His driver drove off.

For the next few minutes Panama took care of his docking duties, signing papers and handing them over to the shipyard's harbor master.

Half an hour later, Jock followed Panama into the captain's cabin.

Jock thought he and Panama had a decent relationship, so he asked, "So, what was going down there? Who were all those people? What was in that orange container?"

The color drained from Panama's ruddy face as he swung around to confront Jock. "What the fuck are you talking about?" Panama's face turned to mottled puce and spittle sprayed the air. His eyes were flat, black and shark-like. "It's none of your business."

Jock realized he'd overstepped the boundaries of their presumed friendship, but he went on. "You know what I'm talking about. That last container. The orange one Chu paid a shitload of cash for."

Panama inhaled deeply and smiled at Jock. "Oh, that was nothing. Just sacks of Columbian coffee beans. You know, those shade-grown yuppie beans those American Starbucks bunnies like." He turned from Jock to indicate the matter was settled.

"My ass." Jock hurled the words at Panama's back, throwing caution to the wind. "No one needs a cadre of heavily armed hoods to protect a Starbucks delivery."

Panama whirled around. His eyes lasered on Jock. "Listen, mate. Best you go to your cabin and forget. I say forget everything you think you saw tonight!" He turned and walked over to the ship's instrument panel.

CHAPTER 57

THE PANAMA CANAL

The ship left the dock at ten, 22:00 hours. The night was still and the sea a surface of glass. The next morning the sun blazed through the small porthole in this cabin. He looked at his watch and saw that it was only a little after 6 AM. After dressing, he walked down to the mess and had breakfast with Captain Panama. Panama did not mention the orange container again and had little else to say.

"We should be dropping anchor within an hour. We have a canal transit booking for 0800 today," said the Captain. "We'll radio to the Cristóbal signal station when we get closer and arrange to meet our pilot. Without a booking, we'd have to wait our turn."

"Panama Canal transit time from east to west should be about twelve hours. My last voyage it took fourteen hours because of construction problems in the Culebra Cut. The Cut is like a valley that runs through the mountains for about eight miles between the locks. In addition to building new, larger locks on the Atlantic and Pacific sides, they need to widen and deepen the Culebra Cut. To do that, it requires blasting and the danger of landslides. When that happens, they have to stop ship movement to clean up. That slows everyone down."

Jock happened to be on the bridge when the pilot and inspectors came aboard after the ship had passed the breakwater. The inspections seemed like a formality. The inspectors disembarked and the pilot took over control of the ship from Panama.

As the ship entered the first set of locks, Jock watched with interest, noting only a couple of feet of free space on either side of the ship. The crew threw lines to workers standing on top of the lock's walls. They attached the lines to electric locomotives. The locomotives traveled with the ship. Their purpose was to keep the ship centered in the locks during its passage.

The ship moved higher through each of the three locks until it reached Gatun Lake, eighty-five feet above sea level. The lines were released. The pilot maneuvered the ship through the lake to the Culebra Cut. The Cut is the most dangerous part of the passage.

Captain Panama said, "Most everyone knows the U.S. built the Panama Canal, but did you know the Frenchies started it?"

"No."

"The Frenchies started work in 1881, but gave up eight years later after wasting a ton of money and losing 22,000 workers. Most of 'em died of malaria and yellow fever. When the U.S. took over, the first thing they did was eradicate the Anopheles mosquitoes. These little bastards carried the diseases."

After passing through the Culebra Cut, the ship entered another lock which lowered the ship to the Mariflores Lake. After two more locks, the ship was at the level of the Pacific Ocean. Travel time had been a little under eleven hours by the time the pilot disembarked.

Panama docked at Port of Balboa on the west side of the Canal and they took on fuel. As soon as the ship's bunkers were topped off with fuel, they departed for New Zealand.

By noon the following day the weather had turned ugly. Midday looked like midnight. Waves crested at twenty-two feet. The water roiled and foamed.

Jock wondered if they ever lost any of the containers in weather like this. He braced himself, one hand on each side of the companionway walls just to remain on his feet. Swaying from side to side threw his stomach into turmoil. He jerked his head over the railing and threw up his breakfast.

To Jock, the ship appeared low in the water. Occasionally, the waves crashed across the bow. He managed to make his way to the bridge. "Hey, Panama. Are we going to get out of this bad weather anytime soon?"

"Not likely. I took her south to avoid the worst of it. That'll add two days to the trip."

After the storm, the voyage was routine. The ship chugged through the water at twenty-two knots. Every evening Jock and Panama played cards and drank and drank more. Chastened by Mother Nature, Jock regretted his decision to go home by sea. It took too long and he missed Grace badly.

CHAPTER 58

SYDNEY, AUSTRALIA

THURSDAY, SEPTEMBER 10, 2015

The Wayward Wind docked in Sydney Harbor on Thursday, September 10, 2015. Immigration and Customs officials came onto the ship.

With nothing to declare, Jock had no issues. Customs was mainly concerned with cargo and gave mere once-overs to the crew and the occasional passenger.

Jesus, it would have been so bloody easy to bring his diamonds back this route. But, where the fuck are they?

He slid his passport across the table to the Customs Official. She scanned it with her hand held portable scanner. After a few seconds of staring at his passport and shaking her head in the negative, she asked Jock, "Your passport must've gotten wet. It won't scan."

"Is that a problem?" Jock's pulse leaped. He inhaled slowly trying to rein back his surging fear.

"No, no. I'll type in the information by hand." She placed the hand-held scanning device on the table and entered the information from Jock's passport. "Ooookay, Mister MacInty. You're good to go. Welcome home."

Once ashore Jock hit a store selling iPhones. He bought one and called home. He imagined the phone ringing in his house in Cairns and Alexa bitching when she looked at the caller ID without knowing who it was. The phone just rang and rang. What happened to voicemail? He shook his head. Bloody Alexa. Where were Adams and Grace? Grace loved to answer phone calls? Next he tried Chu's number. A disembodied voice told him the number had been disconnected. This enraged Jock and confirmed his suspicion that Chu was scamming him. Him, Jock MacInty, formerly Tommy Petroff, King of the Scam.

Jock had read how companies were buying the older smaller container ships and selling them for scrap in Pakistan. They could make a profit quicker by scrapping them than by leasing them out. Maybe that's what the bastard was doing.

Christ, he was glad he hadn't invested that five mill with Chu. The asshole's credibility had been blown from the second Jock spotted him on dock in Columbia doing his dirty drug deal with Panama and those guys with AK-47's.

Getting down and dirty with drug dealers was a totally different ball game than scam artists like himself. I better steer clear of Chu even though he's got my money. Not that Jock was afraid of Chu, he thanked his lucky stars Chu didn't know where he lived.

He breathed a sigh of relief, grateful he'd set up a Trust for Grace, an innocent in all this. Everything I have left is for Grace. She's the only one I care about.

* * *

The taxi from Cairns Airport took an extra fifteen minutes to get to his house, due to a monsoonal downpour. After lugging nothing more than a book on oceanography, bought in Sydney for Grace, Jock hurried up his hilly driveway. The house was in darkness. No pool lights or front door lights. The wind and rain ravaged at his clothes like G forces. He trudged on, his face buried in his chest.

"Alexa, open the bloody door." screamed Jock over the howling rain. "Come on baby. It's me."

Jock rang the front door bell and heard the chime in the house. Then he banged on the door just to piss off Alexa. Nothing. Nada. He stood pounding the door for a few more seconds to no response. He glared around trying to figure out which of the large Jacaranda tree planters held that bloody spare key.

Three planters later, his hand found the key, hidden in a plastic baggie buried in the dirt. The idea to hide the key had been Alexa's. She'd said everybody knew spare keys were under planters but nobody thought to actually find a key buried in one.

As soon as Jock retrieved the key, he threw the dirty, wet, plastic baggie on the ground beside him. Adams could find it tomorrow.

He let himself into his house and fumbled around on the wall to switch on the lights. Nothing moved. The house was eerily silent. An empty silence.

"Adams??!!" screamed Jock. Adams should be around. Nonetheless, no Adams answered Jock. He went from room to room searching for signs of his family. Grace's bedroom was neat and the bed had obviously not been slept in. Adams' room was the same. His and Alexa's bedroom looked like a tornado had passed through, but no sign of Alexa.

His head ached and he stumbled down to the lounge room where his extensive bar awaited. All his bottles of exotic liquors and Knob Creek Whiskey glistened with reflections from the cut crystal glasses. The Knob Creek bottle sat right in the middle of the bar. Jock reached for it. Underneath the bottle he spotted a pale-yellow envelope. Jock poured a hefty glass of Knob Creek before he opened it.

The short and sweet letter instantly galvanized him:

You piece of shit, Jock. You could have told me you weren't coming back. Don't look for me because you'll never find me. You can keep your daughter. You always loved her more than me anyway.

Sayonara Arsehole.

A.

PS. Thanks for the joint account. I closed it with my Montblanc pen.

CHAPTER 59

Jock gulped down his glass of Knob Creek, hastily poured another one, slopping bourbon over the sides of the glass. He threw it back like a man possessed by demons. With the bottle in one hand, he reeled through the kitchen, completely missing the large note held by a magnet on the fridge. He lurched outside. The rain and wind had stopped. A billion stars sparkled. The last phase of the moon glimmered. The clouds had scudded off to rain elsewhere.

Jock smelled the Frangipani blossoms, Grace's favorites. Their scent hung in the air diffuse and pungent.

Where is my precious daughter? Where is Adams? God. Everyone has gone. He slobbered into his drink as he wandered aimlessly to the edge of the pool. He was almost relieved Alexa had gone. Jock was done with her demands. *Good riddance to bad rubbish. I should swear off women.*

Jock clambered up the steps onto the diving board. He hung onto the slim railing of the steps and stared up at the stars. He loved watching Grace on this diving board. She cut into the water like a knife. Jock lowered his head down to look at the water, but a shooting star caught his attention.

"Make a wish." he muttered to himself as the star shot across the night sky.

At that moment, Jock heard a noise behind him. It sounded like deck chairs being moved across the tiles around the pool.

"Who's there? Adams, is that you?" He teetered, trying to keep his balance on the diving board. He put down the bottle and awkwardly turned around on the board.

Standing in the dim moonlight stood his worst nightmare.

"Chu??" Jock was aghast and scared. He rubbed his eyes in disbelief.

Chu held what looked like a pistol in his left hand.

"You loose end, sport. Chu clean up loose end."

Jock felt the wet hair on the back of his neck stand up with an atavistic fear.

"Panama tell me you live here. You think you hide from me?" Chu smirked evilly. "I see you on ship in Cartagena. Not good." Chu racked the slide on the pistol. Snick, Snick. "You not give Chu five mill. Not good."

Jock sobered up immediately. "Hey man, I can get the money. Soon as the banks open."

"Too late. You dead." And Chu pulled the trigger twice.

The first bullet entered his chest just below his collar bone and exited his back, blowing blood and bone matter into the pool. The second bullet found his chest and did not exit. Chu's pistol ejected an empty brass cartridge after each shot. They flew to the right of Chu and made a metallic sound when they landed on the tile pool deck.

Jock felt no pain. Just a rush of air barreling through his chest. The impact of the .40 caliber bullets knocked him off the diving board and into the pool.

His head flung back and he saw another shooting star . . . or was it? His body hit the water with a splat and warm water engulfed him. Grace. Grace. He tried to call out Grace's name, but nothing came out of his mouth. He seemed to soar above his body, above the pool, and he watched as the blood created a dark shadow around his body.

Chu bent to pick up his spent cartridges. As he reached for them, one rolled over the edge into the pool and floated dream-like to the bottom. Chu cursed, dropped the gun and walked away. The gun belonged to Jock. He'd found it in the house. Chu always wore gloves. He waved goodbye at Jock's body and hurried down the driveway to a black limo waiting in the night shadows.

* * *

"Grace, since it's still school holiday, how about you and I drive up to Yepoon for a week or so?" In his head, Adams scrolled through a list of places they could pull their caravan into and camp along the way. "You can see those volcanoes from Rosslyn Bay and we can go to the Capricorn Caves."

"Do you think Mum will come back, Adams? Maybe we should wait a bit to see." Grace poked distractedly through her marine life book. "I don't think she loves me, Adams"

"Yes, she does, Grace. Your Mum loves you. She's just confused in her head and doesn't know how to

282

express her love." Adams didn't want Grace to know she was right in her assessment of her mother. He had no illusions. Alexa was never coming back from her sudden departure to go "shopping in Sydney".

Grace thought a bit then said, "When is Dad coming back? I know he loves me and I love him, Adams." She bit her lip and added, "I love you, too Adams."

"And I love you, too, Grace," Adams quickly tacked on. " . . . So, are we going to go camping on the Capricorn Coast?"

"All right, Adams. Let's camp all the way up the Capricorn Coast. Can we stop off in Rockhampton, too? And go swimming at Emu Park?"

"Pack your bathing costume, girl. We're going to swim every day."

"Hey, Adams, do you know the Capricorn Coast is named after our Tropic of Capricorn which runs through it?"

"Do tell," responded Adams. "Grace, you are such a smart girl." He smiled. His ward was a genius.

The next day Grace and Adams hit the highway. Adams drove the Range Rover, towing a nifty new caravan behind, out of Cairns and headed for Yepoon.

On the east side of the Capricorn Coast was seventy-five kilometers of white sugar-sanded beaches. The shallow waters made for easy wading and swimming. Outcroppings of long extinct volcanoes gave rise to oohs and aahhs from Grace. The Capricorn caves promised more excitement and at the Byfield Range stood a luxuriant rainforest.

By the time they reached Emu Park beach, Grace was tanned as a burnished copper penny and Adams's skin had a reddish, sunburnt glow. Laughing, Grace rolled in sand on the pristine beach then galloped into the water, waving her arms wildly for Adams to follow.

"We'll tell your Dad all about this when he gets back from his trip." called out Adams, immediately wishing he hadn't mentioned anything to Grace about her father. Enthusiastically thrashing in the shallows, Grace appeared not to have heard him.

Adams sighed gratefully as he sloshed through the water some distance behind Grace. Somewhere in the back of his brain, Adams felt a low-level of anxiety blossoming. Right now, though, he did not want to visit those thoughts. That was a dangerous place to ponder unaccompanied.

He just wanted to enjoy these days with Grace.

* * *

Adams and Grace returned a week later from their holiday on the Capricorn Coast.

Grace barreled upstairs not even calling for her Mum. She wanted to check if her father was home.

Meanwhile, Adams looked out the kitchen window to the pool down in the terraced garden.

"Grace." called Adams. "Stay upstairs for a few minutes. OK? I'll bring a surprise up."

His blood ran cold as he dashed down the terraced path to the pool. Jock had been floating for a week.

Adams called Burke, Burke and Wills first, then hurried to call the police.

CHAPTER 60

SAVANNAH, GEORGIA

SATURDAY, AUGUST 22, 2015

The four friends, Dash, Molly, Conor and Meg, met again for drinks and dinner at the Village Bar and Grill on Skidaway Island. After ordering, Conor, in a hushed voice, brought them up to speed on the progress of the investigation.

"The medical examiner placed the time of death between 5 and 7 PM on Wednesday, August 5th. Banderas said he went right from his job at the museum to a fund raiser at the Westin. He claims he was there until after ten and took a taxi home because he had a lot to drink. He and Laura have separate bedrooms, so he didn't notice she wasn't home when he went to bed. His alibi checked out. That eliminates him as a suspect."

"Merilee's alibi checked out too. She drove home, changed, and then went to a friend's house for dinner and Canasta. They played Canasta until shortly before ten."

"I looked back at our incident reports and found that Laura Banderas called security about a possible home invasion back in June." Dash added. She said she was sure someone had been in her house. Nothing was missing but her lap top had been moved and there were grass clippings on the floor by the sliding glass doors."

Conor continued, "We looked at the surveillance videos from Merrill Lynch. They were not helpful because the camera encompassed a very limited area, just the door on the library's new wing. At 5:32 the video showed a man exiting from that door. He scuttled through the rain. Another man followed on his heels."

"Merilee said Laura was the only one in the Library when she left a little before 5. The rain was coming down so hard we couldn't get a good ID of either man from the Merrill Lynch camera. But we did get a clear shot of the license plate on the car the first man left in."

"Here's where things start to get very murky. We identified the car as the same car that went off the bridge the night of the murder. It was rented by someone named Jock MacInty from Australia. The driver was never found. We looked for fingerprints in the car, but they had been washed away. The lab boys are still going over the car. We couldn't get much on MacInty. His credit cards showed that he checked into the Hyatt downtown back in June and checked out the day of the murder. Other than that, we found practically nothing on MacInty."

"There are the fingerprints on that statue. We had no trouble lifting a clear set of prints because of the blood. Laura's blood. We ran the prints and couldn't find anything at first. Until we checked the Federal database and we got a hit . . . a very old hit. The prints on the statue belong to someone who worked part time for the US Postal Service in the 70's. But the owner of the prints died in China in 1994."

Molly's felt goose bumps on her arms. She asked, "Who's fingerprints were they?"

"A guy by the name of Tommy Petroff. Why?" asked Conor.

"Tommy Petroff? Are you sure?"

"Yes, why?"

"Tommy Petroff!" exclaimed Molly. "Tommy Petroff was married to Laura Banderas before she came down here. My late husband, Bob, worked for Tommy Petroff's company before he died mysteriously in D.C. back in 1992. I even paid for an advanced toxicology screen. It turned up nothing. Remember Dash? That's where we first met. Dash investigated Bob's death."

"We found nothing suspicious." Dash interjected.

"I kind of remember Tommy disappearing in China on a business trip right before all of his companies crashed. I don't think his body was ever found. The Feds thought Tommy was running a Ponzi scheme. It was all in all the papers for weeks after he died. They said a lot of people lost money in Tommy's scheme. Many law suits were filed by investors trying to get their money back. Some money was recovered but most of it had vanished. The news stories reported Laura was able to retain the mansion in Greenwich and life insurance. Eventually, after the publicity died down, I remember he was declared dead and Laura moved down here with Javier. I might be wrong. It was all so long ago."

She paused and then continued, "I never knew what to think about the charges against Tommy. That wasn't the Tommy I remember. I liked him from the first time we met at a dinner in his home in Greenwich. He was very kind to me after Bob died. I really have a hard time believing he was behind a scheme to defraud all of those people. But we'll never know. He died before the Feds exposed the alleged scheme.

WEDNESDAY, SEPTEMBER 9, 2015

Merilee fidgeted. So much had happened. No one, neither that Dash Santorelli, nor the Detective, whatever-his-name was, asked Merilee about diamonds. She had told them all the truth . . . well, a version of the truth or . . . as close to the truth as she could. The word diamonds was never mentioned. She hoped they didn't notice her sweaty palms.

Laura was dead as dead could be. Javier, bless his artsy heart, was inconsolable. He told her the police were still calling him with questions. She sees the Landings Security car cruising past her house. But maybe it's Javier's house their watching.

She had Javier for dinner at least two times a week, always catered unbeknown to him. Despite the loss of his wife, the man ate like a horse.

Mi amore, my Laura, my Laura, he kept blubbering all over Merilee's table as he scarfed up the curried quail with lightly sautéed brussel sprouts from Whole Foods.

"You know, Merilee, Nietzsche said when you looka ina the abyss for ze long time, the abyss is looka back at you." Javier's accent blurred as he snorted and stuffed a forkful of quail into his mouth. Since Laura is gone, I'm looka ina ze abyss all ze time."

Merilee gazed adoringly at the centerpiece.

"Who's Neetcha?" Merilee asked coyly. Most times she didn't have a clue what Javier was talking about. He seemed like a man wallowing in grief, while still trying to keep his strength up. She could fix that issue for as long as he wanted. He seemed content to visit her. Now on to phase two of her plan.

"Nietzsche isa ze God of alla knowledge," Javier answered firmly. He leaned forward over his plate and inhaled the scent of his food, his chin almost brushing it.

"Oh, yes, a Greek god. I remember those from a course I took. All about what gods are in charge of what." Merilee blithely answered. "I invented a Parking Goddess who can secure me prime parking places anywhere. Her name is Barbara Duvane. More quail, Javier?"

"You come downtown to mi studio tomorrow, Merry. I makea you ze perfect sculpture," Javier crooned after his last mouthful. He stood, pushing the chair back. He left his empty plate on the dining room table and his chair three feet away. "I see you later, ma petite chou." He added as he headed for the front door.

"Javier, what time do . . ?" The door closed sharply. Great. Now I don't know what time to meet him. Nonetheless, Merilee couldn't stop looking at her centerpiece. She would leave at 11 tomorrow morning right after the maid came. The woman had been coming once a month for years and Merilee trusted her, within reason. Once she had washed the rugs on the porch and broken the washing machine. Merilee said no more rugs, mats, or carpets in the washing machine.

The next morning Merilee paced in front of the window waiting for the maid. And here she was, walking up the driveway. Two minutes late, but Merilee wouldn't say anything about that today. Fournier and Fredericka were on the dining room table licking Javier's dirty plate.

290

"Fournier, Fredericka, come." Both leaped off the table. She put the squirming fuzz-balls in their ferret-friendly room with all the luxuries a ferret could want.

"Nonie, I'm going out now, so just lock up when you leave." Merilee's parting words to the maid. She went to her garage, got into her car, and left to meet Javier.

CHAPTER 61

Nonie, short, plump and Chinese-American, loved cleaning up. Even as a child she'd been obsessive-compulsive. Everything in its place, and a place for everything. That was her motto. She'd been doing Landings houses for twenty years now. House siting, pet watching, cleaning house, and elder care when necessary. Word of mouth gave her the best reputation anyone could have. She'd earned it.

Some clients were a bit more demanding which was fine too. All she said was, "Yes Ma'am." and that was that. She remembered last week she'd had to bathe Doctor Molly's big poodle because the dog had rolled in deer poop and chewed on something dead and rotting on her daily walk. Even being on a leash couldn't prevent Stella from rolling in foul-smelling things.

"Oh Nonie, if you could just shower Stella with her special soap I'd be so grateful. She stinks worse than day-old doody and I have to meet Dash for lunch in ten minutes."

"No problem, Doctor Molly. She'll be clean and sweat smelling when you come home." Nonie walked Stella to the shower in the guest suite. Stella was half as tall as Nonie, but much more affectionate than Miss Merilee's awful ferrets. Nonie ignored them.

Today when Nonie arrived at Miss Merilee's house she left those nasty ferrets with sharp little teeth locked up in their room. She picked up the dirty dishes on the dining room table when out of nowhere, one of the ferrets shot past her legs scaring the daylights out of her. Nonie lost her balance. The dirty plates started to slip out of her hand and she lurched to save the plates, catching her elbow on the lip of the Kosta Boda glass bowl. The entire magnolia centerpiece tumbled off the table and smashed onto the Italian tiled floor.

"No. No. Noooo!" screamed Nonie and quickly looked out the window to make sure Miss Merilee was already gone.

The bowl had smashed into a million pieces and all those clear glass marbles were rolling around mixed in with the shards and splinters of the crystal bowl. She immediately retrieved the fake magnolias and leaves. Then she dashed to the laundry where she snatched up a broom and dustpan. Ten minutes later she'd swept up all the broken glass and marbles. She deposited the mess into a plastic bag and, as luck would have it, the trash people were walking up the side of the house for a trash pick-up.

I'm lucky just when I need it thought Nonie.

After half an hour of searching through closets, Nonie found a glass bowl high on a shelf that looked about the same size as the broken one. Plus, this bowl already had glass marbles in it. Lucky again.

Her arrangement with the magnolia leaves looked so much like the other one, Nonie had to smile a smile of relief. She was sure Miss Merilee wouldn't be mad at her when she called tomorrow and explained what happened.

The rest of the house cleaning proved uneventful. Uneventful because those furry rodents didn't appear at any time and Nonie did not approach their room from which they had clearly found a way out.

She left about 2 PM and drove her pale blue Sonata over to Doctor Molly's house which would take her no time to clean. Only the dog, Stella, made the messes. She chewed electrical cords, garden hoses, book covers, shoes, and paper towels, but Doctor Molly took care of that. If Stella were a human, she would be Doctor Molly's favorite child.

Nonie called Merilee the next day blubbering about something. Merilee couldn't understand a word she'd said. Something about the ferrets being loose. But Fournier and Fredericka were both fine. She was sure Nonie would tell her when she came next week

MONDAY, SEPTEMBER 14, 2015

"Mr. Banderas?"

"Yes."

"Mr. Godfrey Templeton the Second will see you now. Please follow me."

Javier rose from his chair, pulled down his suit coat, straightened his tie, and followed the woman never taking his eyes off her ample hips.

"Hello, Mr. Banderas." said a distinguished man with short gray hair and a narrow mustache. "Please have a seat."

Javier carefully sat down in an uncomfortable antique chair. "Mr. Templeton, I come about my deceased wife's estate. She never confide in me about her money and things. I know you are Laura's attorney since she move here eleven year ago before we married."

"That is correct. I prepared her will. Although it has not yet been filed with the probate court, I am free to tell you in general how she intended to distribute her assets."

Javier smiled, folded his hands on his lap, and tried to repress his excitement.

"Your wife had several investment accounts, largely in negotiable stocks and bonds. After taxes these will amount to approximately $400,000. She bequeathed these funds to Boston University to establish the Laura Higginbottom scholarship for deserving young women."

"But she never finished university!" exclaimed Javier.

"True, but she confided in me that she always had fond feelings for Boston University because that is where she met her first husband, Tommy."

"What else?" Said Javier becoming more daunted by the minute.

"She left you the house and the personal property, including her jewelry and her car."

"But ze money? None?"

"I'm afraid not Mr. Banderas." Mr. Templeton rose from the chair behind his desk and said, "I am sorry for your losses. If that will be all, I am quite busy. I will notify you when the estate is settled. Good bye."

Shoulders slumping, Javier stood, turned, opened the door and left without another word. Bitch! he thought.

That evening, Javier feasted on Paella Merilee had wheedled out of a private chef. She stared adoringly at Javier who sat opposite her almost hidden by the magnolia centerpiece. She moved her head slightly to the side of the centerpiece when she noticed, quite unconsciously, the glass balls in the bowl were a pale blue. Not clear. The shape of the bowl struck her as not right also. It took all of thirty seconds for Merilee to realize she was looking at a completely different bowl.

She stood up suddenly, knocking her chair with such force it toppled over backwards.

"Oh. My. God!" was all Merilee could hiss as her hands flew to her mouth.

"Merry, this Paella is fantastic," mumbled Javier, his face inches from his plate as he shoveled lumps of fish into his mouth. Javier was blissfully unaware of Merilee's horror.

It took all of Merilee's strength and composure not to scream. She felt the blood drain from her head and pool in her feet.

"Merry, you unwell?" Javier finally asked. He'd stopped chewing Paella and just stared at Merilee.

"Yes, yes. I just remembered I have to cook a dish for my church for tomorrow morning. You don't mind if I cut short our evening?" Merilee needed to get rid of him. She had to check out the bowl and find the diamonds.

"Si. Si. But you look so pale, mi amore. Can I help?"

"No. No. No, I'm fine," Merilee hissed. "I'll see you . . . tomorrow.

CHAPTER 62

WEDNESDAY, NOVEMBER 11, 2015

The two couples were having dinner and the subject of the murder arose.

Conor told them, "Whoever was driving the red car, whether it was Jock MacInty or someone else, we never found a body. But we did find a tracking device attached to the rear bumper. We traced the device using its serial number to an electronics shop in Jacksonville. We found out that it had been purchased by a fellow named Lester Mazza."

"Wait a minute," said Molly. "I seem to remember that name. There was a Les Mazza at Petroff Enterprises. In fact, I think he was the security guy who took Bob to the airport when he went to D.C."

Conor continued, "Dash and I drove down to Jacksonville to interview Mazza. As we walked up to his door Dash noticed a pickup truck in the driveway. It had a bar code on the window similar to the ones issued by the Landings Association to allow people into the gated community. Dash wrote down the number. He called his office and found out it had been stolen off a Comcast van in June. That gave us something more to talk to Mazza about."

"Our interview with Mazza didn't last long. We questioned him about the tracking device, the bar code sticker, and his whereabouts at the time of the murder. We got nothing. That's when he lawyered up."

Dash added, "But what we had was enough to get a search warrant. Once we got our hands on his smart phone, we could see who he had called and where he had been. He had been in Savannah near the library on the day Laura was murdered and he crossed the same bridge as the red car.

When we searched Laura's house we dusted for prints. We found Mazza's prints in her house. He could have broken into her house back in June about the time that a Comcast truck with the same Landings sticker was reported stolen. We can't come up with a motive, but Mazza could have killed Laura. The evidence against him is all circumstantial, but may be enough to put him away for a while."

Dash said, "Conor, do you think Mazza had something to do with Bob Hathaway's death in D.C?"

"Dash, that was so long ago. We don't have any evidence connecting Mazza to Bob." said Conor.

WEDNESDAY, DECEMBER 23, 2015

Merilee wanted to get as far away as she could from lost diamonds, murder and incompetent maids. She sold her house. The buyer wanted to close as fast as possible.

Merilee did a little jig amidst her furry twosome, Fournier and Fredericka. She might have lost the diamonds, but she still had her divorce settlement to comfort her. After losing the diamonds Merilee fired Nonie with gusto.

Merilee winced as she recalled Nonie saying, "Miss Merilee, sorry I broke your bowl but I clean up all the glass."

"Where is it?" Merilee asked.

"Trash man took all glass away. Floor all clean. Ferrets not get glass in paws."

"Yes. Yes. I understand," began Merilee containing her absolute fury. "I just can't afford to keep you, Nonie. I'll call you when I need you. No more once a week. I'll call you. Do you understand?" Merilee's lips pursed like cement had been poured on them. Anger surged through her.

After selling the house, starting anew was Merilee's main focus.

The Landings was history. She'd go to Saint Elsewhere . . . somewhere down in Florida. She didn't care who got murdered in the Village Library, as long as she was far, far away.

Well, not really. Despite not liking Laura, Merilee felt the tug of remorse. Nobody deserved a fate at the hand of that weird fellow they'd booked for the murder. Yuk. He looked familiar though. They'd posted his mug shot in the Savannah Morning News. When she saw his pock-marked face, she remembered seeing him. It had been a few days before Laura's murder. He'd been getting out of a Comcast van parked in front of Javier's and Laura's house. The man walked up the driveway as though he had an appointment at the house. She thought nothing of it even when she saw the van the very next night and knew Javier was down in Sarasota. Well, maybe Laura had been home that night.

"Oh Fredericka," purred Merilee, distracted from her thoughts on that man. "What have you brought to your mommy?"

The ferret nudged and smooched at Merilee's ankles. She was pushing a toy into Merilee's foot. This was what Fredericka always did when she wanted attention. Merilee picked up the toy and threw it. The ferret dashed after it, scooped it up in her mouth and padded back to Merilee.

She swept up the ball of twine in one hand, readying her arm for another throw when she felt something hard buried in the side of the twine ball. She peered at the twine and pried out whatever was half buried within. "Oh, My God! It's one of my diamonds." She gazed down at what must be at least a three or four carat diamond. "My diamond!" She exclaimed.

301

* * *

"Javier. Javier. My darling boy, I have a treat for us," Merilee gushed on the phone. "Just come over so I can show it to you. We can go to The Olde Pink House for dinner if you like. I've just come into some cold hard cash." Cold and hard was exactly the right description. Merilee would show Javier her diamond.

"*Si, mia amore*," said Javier using his deeply accented voice for Merilee. She had grown on him since Laura passed. "I come now . . . five minutes. Give me time to slip on my Guccis." Merilee had bought him these loafers which were exceedingly comfortable.

"I have something to tell you too." Javier had decided to marry Merilee and take her down to Sarasota. The Sarasota area teamed with Europeans and South Americans. He already had commissions enough to open up a studio down there.

After his Laura had been slaughtered right there in the Village Library, Javier's life improved . . . through no fault of his own.

The little woman next door cooked like Gaudi's private chef and she seemed very serious about her highway to Javier's heart.

Ayee! The rent on his Charleston Gallery had gone up so much; he'd not renewed the lease. In the meantime, a commission for a life size bronze had come to him from Sarasota. He'd gone down there to make nice with his patron (a Brazilian billionaire with a penchant for art) and one thing led to another. This would be the first time he had ever actually kept a woman as opposed to being kept by a woman.

Laura, in a moment of wifely generosity, had bequeathed her Landings house in Deer Creek to him. And the detective Donovan had returned all of Laura's belongings to him, her clothes, the iPad and that huge diamond ring. He had to still decide whether to cash it in or give it to Merry as an engagement ring.

He would make another statue of a child reading, reminiscent of the earlier stature which Laura had loved so much. When he mentioned he would give the old statue to Merilee, Laura had professed her attachment to it. He would never have given it to Merilee after Laura told him how she'd loved it, but she should not have given it to the library. Now, he'd make another one as a tribute to his dear, generous Laura.

* * *

Molly and Dash were sitting on a swing on the rear deck of Molly's house. As the sun set, the clouds over the marsh blazed in a rainbow of pinks and reds. What made the evening perfect was the absence of sand gnats. Stella was running around on the lawn below. Dash had fired up Molly's grill. He had picked up some steaks from Smith Brothers' Butcher shop in downtown Savannah.

He had his arm around Molly. They both sipped wine, a red they'd found on a weekend trip to north Georgia. The wine was called Centurio, a mix of 60%

Cabernet Sauvignon and 40% Merlot grown and bottled at the Montaluce vineyard near Dahlonega, Georgia. The restaurant where they had enjoyed a lunch and a dinner overlooked the vineyard spread out below.

Molly was unusually quiet.

"Is your wine okay? Are you feeling alright?" asked Dash.

Molly paused and then said, "I'm just thinking about all that has happened, the bad and the good. If Bob and I had never gone to dinner at Petroff's house in Greenwich, Bob would never have been hired by Tommy. If he had never worked for Petroff, he wouldn't have been in D.C. where he was killed. Then there is Laura's murder. Every time I set foot in the hall at the library or look at that statue resting on the bookshelf I see her lying in a pool of blood. I never cared for Laura from the first time I met her. I don't think she liked me much either, but I surely didn't want her to be murdered."

"If all that bad stuff hadn't happened we wouldn't be sitting here tonight. This is the good part."

"I just don't understand why Mazza would kill Laura. And I don't understand how Tommy Petroff's prints could have gotten on that statue. Do you think that Tommy might still be alive?"

"I doubt it. There is no record of Petroff returning to the U.S. after his well-publicized death in China."

"Perhaps you're right. It's over now. I need to think about the good and not the bad."

I'm hungry. Let's grill those steaks."

CHAPTER 63

THURSDAY, MARCH 17, 2016

Truth be told, the only people downtown in Savannah on St. Patrick's Day were out of town tourists, visiting policemen and firemen from Chicago, New York, and Ireland . . . and those who marched enthusiastically in the parade. Everyone downtown was in high spirits, literally.

Dash and Molly opted to watch the St. Patrick's Day parade on TV from the comfort of Molly's sitting room. Molly made brief forays into the kitchen to work on her contribution to the St. Patrick's Day dinner at Conor's and Megan's that evening, assuming they were still able to host it after their marching and frolicking.

Dash shouted to Molly in the kitchen, "Hurry. Come here. I see them."

Molly grabbed a dish towel to dry her hands and rushed in and plopped down on the sofa beside Dash. Conor and Megan, along with the entire O'Kelley clan were marching down Broughton Street. They all wore the same white tee shirts on which were emblazoned the words "The Luck of the Irish To Ya!"

"Oh, that looks like such fun, doesn't it, Dash?"

"Not really. I would much rather be here with you and Stella, with my feet up and drinking my Bloody Mary. Where's yours?"

"In the kitchen. I'll get it."

"The next thing Dash heard was "NO. NO. OH, NO!"

Dash raced to the kitchen and did his utmost not to smile as he saw on the floor, the remains of the soft pretzels Molly had placed on the countertop to cool. Stella had only eaten two of them, but the remaining pretzels were not fit for human consumption now.

Molly glared as she watched Stella slink to her bed and curl up for a nap.

"Stella was just celebrating St. Patrick's Day. Too bad she didn't have any of that special mustard we bought to dip the pretzels in. Don't worry, sweetie. We'll think of another German appetizer to honor your heritage, Ms. Cohen. How about I pick up some Bratwursts? I'll grill them and cut them up in bite-sized pieces. I'll bring them with me when I come to pick you up in a few hours. How about 4:30?"

"Don't be mad at Stella. As a trained law enforcement officer, it's my opinion that you were an aider and an abettor in this crime." He leaned down, kissed the top of her head, and went out the door whistling, "When Irish Eyes Are Smiling."

* * *

At the Donovans, they found both Megan and Connor in the dining room setting the table. The crystal and silver gleamed in the light of the chandelier, and the center-piece was a sight to behold. Several dozen emerald

306

green carnations were amassed in a large globe-shaped glass vase.

"Megan! Those are gorgeous. Where did you find them?" Molly asked.

"Ask that swell fella standing behind you", Megan grinned. "You are too much, Dash. You always do the nicest things."

Connor pretended to harrumph, "Yeah, ain't he the best? Molly keeps telling me to take a few tips from him."

Dash went to the kitchen and deposited his dessert offering in the refrigerator and Molly followed with her chafing dish of bratwurst. "Where shall I put these, Megan?"

"Let's have drinks in the den by the fireplace." Megan suggested. "It got a bit breezy by the end of the parade and we thought a fire would take the chill out of our bones. Why don't you put the sausages and mustard on the coffee table?"

Drinks in hand, they all moved to the den. As Connor stirred the logs in the fire, Dash said, "Did you both come home and crash for a few hours after all of the fun?"

"I came home and took a shower after all those strangers kissing and hugging me." Megan sighed. "Conor was out like a light on the sofa when I got out of the shower, so I laid myself down on the bed for a nap. As I nodded off, the phone rang. It was my son Robbie. My kids always make a big deal out of St. Paddy's Day. Robby told us all about the parade he marched in up in Athens with his buddies. He's really enjoying life there.

He is so proud to be a second-year police officer. He's like his Dad in so many ways."

"Then, as soon as we hung up with Robbie, Katy called. She's living in Dahlonega now and teaching English and creative writing in the high school there. Her big news is that she met the 'most handsome guy'. He works at a big, fancy winery outside of town and is charge of the chemical part of winemaking. I don't really understand it all, but his job is very important according to Katy and she asked if she could bring him to our big Fourth of July party this summer."

"Wait a minute," Conor interjected. "This sounds serious. She's only twenty-seven."

"And, how old were we when we married, Mr. Donovan?"

Conor looked to the ceiling and grinned.

Dash cleared the plates and returned with his dessert offering. "I figured that after our German appetizer and Megan's terrific Irish dinner we needed a taste of Italy to complete our International St. Patrick's Day dinner. Tiramisu anyone?"

Coffee, with a nip of Irish whisky, was poured, amidst groans of contentment from each diner.

"Molly, I think we had best head home while we're still able. I'm so happy and sated I'm almost asleep."

Dash turned into Molly's drive and she turned to him. "Are you too sleepy for a nightcap?"

"Never too sleepy for a nightcap with you."

"Follow me, Detective. I'll let Stella out and light the fire."

Settling in the living room by the fire, Molly broke the silence. "I wonder . . ."

"What do you wonder?"

"Well, I was just thinking about Megan and Conor. Their lives seem so full and rich. And . . ."

"And what, Molly?"

"Did you ever wish you had children?"

"Aren't you happy, Molly?"

"Of course I am. You make me extremely happy. I love my work and volunteer activities, but it crossed my mind to wonder what it would be like if I had had children."

Dash drew her to him and gave her a hug. "Molly Cohen, I love you exactly the way you are. Aren't Stella and I enough of a family for you?"

CHAPTER 64

SATURDAY, OCTOBER 8, 2016

Dash came in the back door and tossed Molly's mail on the kitchen counter.

"I'm getting a beer. Do you want one?"

"Yes, please." Molly replied as she opened an envelope.

Dash set her beer down and stared at her.

"Molly, are you all right? You're white as a ghost."

"Funny you should use that term. I'm reading a letter about a ghost."

"What are you talking about?"

"Here. Read this for yourself." Molly handed the letter to Dash.

He hesitantly took the letter from Molly. It was hand written on heavy, cream-colored parchment in blue ink, the cursive writing had an elegant, flowing look. Dash recalled cursive wasn't taught in schools anymore. The letter seemed to come from another era.

Dash began to read.

Ian Adams

October 1st, 2016

7 Coogee Lane

Cairns, Queensland, 1234
Australia

Dear Dr. Cohen,

My name is Ian Adams. For the
last eleven years I have been employed as a
Major-Domo for a man by the name of Jock
MacInty. I live in Cairns, Australia.

Mr. MacInty was murdered in his
home on September 10th of this year. He has
a daughter, Grace, who was born October 17,
2006.

Grace's mother left Mr. MacInty.
She made it clear she wanted nothing to do with
the child.

Before his death, Mr. MacInty set up a trust for Grace. I am named Grace's primary guardian and trustee.

This may come as a shock. You are named as guardian and trustee in the event I become incapacitated or unable to perform the legalities of said trust.

Mr. MacInty told me he had great faith in you.

Dash paused to look at Molly. "Who the hell is Jock MacInty?"

"Keep reading." said Molly staring out the window. The first drops of rain started spitting from the grey, billowy sky.

Dash read on.

After Mr. MacInty set up the trust for Grace, he confided in me that Jock MacInty

312

was not his given name. He informed me he was a businessman from the United States of America and that his true name was Tommy Petroff.

"Is this some kind of joke, Molly?" asked Dash. "Tommy Petroff Enterprises? The guy who ran the huge Ponzi scheme back in the nineties? The guy who purportedly died in China? The very same guy we thought may have driven his car off the Skidaway Bridge a few months ago? How could he have been murdered in Australia if he died in China? Your late husband, Bob, worked for him, right?"

Molly sat silent. She continued to stare out the window. Now the rain pelted noisily again the glass.

Dash kept reading.

I do not have any medical issues at this time. I feel it would do Grace an injustice not to meet you while we are all well. I am hoping of course, your health is good.

I know nothing about you except Mr. MacInty trusted you as he trusted me. With that in mind, I wonder if you would care to come to Cairns to meet Grace. If you are willing to visit, the trust will pay your plane fare and sundry expenses.

I know you will love Grace as I do.

Sincerely,
Ian Adams

P.S. You can reach me at our house telephone number, 16174032214 for any other information you deem necessary.

Dash gently placed the letter on the table. "Molly? Will you go?"

Molly turned from the window and walked over to Dash. "Yes, of course I'll go. I want to meet Ian Adams and Grace MacInty." A tear found a path down her cheek. "I know it is weird Dash, but I feel a connection because I knew Tommy."

ABOUT THE AUTHORS

Victoria Collett

Victoria Collett is currently an Operating Room nurse purportedly retired, but working nonetheless. She has tendrils in a slew of different areas which include watercolor painting, writing, birding and a whiff of gardening just to keep her hummingbirds coming back for more and the raccoons retreating in horror.

Robert Fogarty

Robert Fogarty retired after thirty years as a corporate lawyer. He retired after twelve years as a high handicap golfer. He retired after 5 years as president of The Village Library. Now he spends time planning his next trip to Walt Disney World.

Corinne Webner

Corinne Webner taught elementary school music, middle school and high school English. As a therapeutic adjunct to rearing three young children, she enrolled in law school and subsequently practiced trademark and copyright law. Now retired from those amusing and intriguing pastimes, she watches the tides ebb and flow and leads a contemplative life with great delight.